SECRET
PORTLAND
OREGON

2010 EDITION

SECRET
PORTLAND
OREGON

The Unique Guidebook
to Portland's Hidden Sites,
Sounds, & Tastes

2010 EDITION

Ann Carroll Burgess

AND

Tom Burgess

WITH PHOTOGRAPHS BY
Linda Rutenberg

ECW PRESS

NATIONAL LIBRARY OF CANADA CATALOGUING IN PUBLICATION DATA

Burgess, Ann Carroll
Secret Portland, Oregon 2010 : the unique guidebook
to Portland's hidden sites, sounds, & tastes / Ann Carroll Burgess and Tom Burgess.

(Secret guides)
Includes index.
ISBN 978-1-55022-924-0

1. Portland (Or.)--Guidebooks. I. Burgess, Tom
II. Title. III. Series: Secret guides

F884.P83B87 2009   917.95'490444   C2009-906288-7

Original series design: Paul Davies / Series editor: Laura Byrne Paquet
Typesetting: *Martel en-tête* / Imaging: Guylaine Régimbald – SOLO DESIGN /
Cover Design: Tania Craan / Cover Image: iStockPhoto
Printing: Webcom   1   2   3   4   5

Mixed Sources
Product group from well-managed
forests, and other controlled sources
FSC   www.fsc.org Cert no. SW-COC-002358
© 1996 Forest Stewardship Council

Published by ECW PRESS
2120 Queen Street East, Suite 200, Toronto, Ontario M4E 1E2
416.694.3348 / info@ecwpress.com

The publication of *Secret Portland, Oregon* has been generously supported by the
Government of Canada through the Book Publishing Industry Development Program.

Canadä

PRINTED AND BOUND IN CANADA

ECW PRESS
ecwpress.com

TABLE OF CONTENTS

SECRET...

ACKNOWLEDGMENTS

A book of this range is never a solo effort. Without the generous help of so many friends, family, and business associates it would not contain as many "secrets" as are held within these covers.

I'd particularly like to thank Deborah Wakefield of the Portland Oregon Visitors Association, Lila Martin of Travel Portland, Julie Gangler of the Washington County Visitor Association, Sarah Biggerstaff, David Spacek, Dina Nishikoa, and Alice Freuler of the West Columbia Gorge Chamber of Commerce.

And to my family members who gave up their secrets to the city, a special thanks to Robert Curtis, Melissa Wellin, Barbara and Abner Sweeting, William Curtis, Dolly and Gerry Freeman, Michael Curtis, Patricia Curtis, Mark Curtis, Richard Curtis, and David Walker.

INTRODUCTION

Just imagine a city where a bookstore occupies an entire municipal block. A city where the art of brewing beer has been reborn. A city of the world's smallest dedicated park and the largest forested city wilderness. Well, you would have to be imagining Portland.

Portland is not what you expect. It is not a smaller version of Seattle. Oh, there are some similarities — both have water, both have mountains. One has moved constantly forward with new architecture, freeways, and high-tech industries. That's Seattle. Portland, on the other hand, has kept most of its heritage architecture, built one of the finest public transport systems anywhere, and lured its own share of industry. Like all good siblings, the two have similarities and differences. It's the differences that make Portland so special.

Built more on a European model, Portland is a walker's nirvana. The city's streets, which feature statues, fountains, and half-size city blocks, were part of the reason why Portland was selected by *Walking* magazine as one of America's best walking cities. Some historians claim that these people-friendly city blocks were the invention of greedy real estate developers who wanted to create more corner lots, which fetched higher prices. Others, however, believed that the shorter blocks were created to allow more natural light to fall down to street level.

Whatever the reason, when you are confronted with what appears to be a 20-block walk, relax, breathe deeply, and know that your next destination is closer than you think.

Portland has kept its residents in mind as it has evolved. During its modern era, from the close of World War II, the city has added such utopian refinements as an extensive transit system and an urban plan that strictly limits the height of buildings and the space between them.

Bridges also give Portland a distinct profile, covering the city like a latticework over the Willamette River. This riverfront city is a multi-faceted place. Like the confluence of the Willamette and the Columbia Rivers, commerce, history, classic architecture, and the arts come together smoothly to create a flourishing metropolis.

Portland is much more than its physical attributes. The city has a progressive beat, even if the drummer keeps the cadence slow and steady. This is a city that knows how to make the best of its sunny days, from the numerous sidewalk cafés and outdoor festivals to the passion for gardening.

And gardening truly is a passion in the Northwest. "Grow it" and "show it" seem to be the bywords, not just for the ever-present roses, but also for swarms of rhododendrons, squadrons of perennials, and legions of trees.

That outdoor passion, along with having the head office of Nike in the backyard, has certainly added to the city's zeal for sports. Snowboarding and skiing are doable almost all year long on Mount Hood; the rivers offer boating, water skiing, and fishing opportunities; and the hiking trails are almost too numerous to mention.

Need some more reasons why Portland is such a great place? Let's see. No sales tax, old-fashioned gas stations, the only extinct volcano within city limits in the United States, clean air, an excellent transit system. I could go on and on, but then there wouldn't be any point in writing the rest of this book.

When trying to find an address, it's wise to think of the city in terms of quadrants: northwest, north/northeast, southeast, and southwest. Numbered avenues are parallel and run north-south, with street addresses starting from Burnside Street, which divides north and south. Named streets are also parallel and run east-west, with the Willamette (which divides east and west) at zero. But, to be honest with you, while the grid system and coordinates make finding an address easy, most people know the city by its neighborhoods.

So come and explore. Just make sure that you take time to watch the weather machine in Pioneer Courthouse Square, choose a favorite blossom at the International Rose Test Garden, ride the only three-door elevator west of the Mississippi, take a pub crawl among the microbreweries, and hobnob with the artists on the first or last Thursday of the month.

HOW TO USE SECRET PORTLAND

This book is arranged alphabetically, by subject. If you're a jazz aficionado, flip to "Secret Jazz"; if you're a bohemian at heart, turn to "Secret Boho." Craving a meal from a faraway place? Try "Secret Irish," "Secret Japanese," or "Secret Italian." Need to wander among stalls of vegetables and crafts? Look for "Secret Markets."

With each location, we provide you with a phone number and an address. The 503 area code has been included with all the numbers to remind you that within the city you must use the area code. The address also includes the neighborhood (Mount Tabor or Sabin, for instance). If the site is outside Portland, we also include "Oregon" (or, in rare instances, "Washington"). You won't find hours or directions unless there is something unique about them. Since restaurants and clubs have a propensity for moving or closing, we recommend that you call ahead before visiting, just to make sure the operation is still in operation. Most of this book is devoted to Portland and its surrounding areas, but it also includes just a few absolutely irresistible entertainments beyond the city limits.

And don't forget to peruse "Secret Periodicals." Here, you will find a list of all the free newspapers that provide up-to-the-minute information about happenings around town. "Secret Web Sites" will let you do some homework before your trip, or while you are here, on location in the City of Roses.

SECRET

ABORIGINAL

When Lewis and Clark first arrived at the mouth of the Columbia River (present-day Astoria), over 200 years ago — in 1805, to be precise — the Willamette Valley and Columbia Gorge were home to dozens of Native American tribes.

Multnomah County is named for the tribe that once occupied the Portland area. In the ensuing years, most tribes lost their land and economic strength to the newcomers. Today, they're gaining some of it back through casino revenues. Two of the largest casinos are near the Oregon Coast — **Spirit Mountain** (Grande Ronde, Oregon, 800-760-7977, www.spiritmountain.com) and **Chinook Winds** (Lincoln City, Oregon, 888-CHINOOK, www.chinookwindscasino.com).

If you're more interested in the past than in the present cha-ching of the slot machines, head to the Oregon History Center (see "Secret History") for its fine collection of more than 1,000 photographic images, as well as basketry, beadwork, leatherwork, and stone items from many Northwest tribes.

SECRET

AERIAL

The newest addition to Portland's creative ways of seeing the city will lift you to new heights. The **Aerial Tram** (www.portlandtram .org) will take you from South Waterfront Street to Marquam Hill, traveling some 3,300 linear feet and rising in elevation by 500 feet.

The tram is owned by Portland Transit but was built to address the expansion of the Marquam Campus of Oregon Health Sciences University and to provide easier access to the already existing facilities.

Designed and manufactured in Switzerland, the tram was built to handle local seismic concerns and any unusual weather that the city might experience, such as the infrequent ice storms.

The best part of the tram is that it connects with the streetcar system so you won't have to worry about finding a parking place for your bike or your car.

SECRET

AFRICA

The Horn of Africa (3939 NE Martin Luther King Jr. Boulevard, King, 503-331-9844, www.hornofafrica.net) is small and bright and personable. This tiny restaurant features East African cuisine, highly influenced by Indian touches. The meat dishes are tender and the complex appetizers are well worth a try. Not too far away, the **Queen of Sheba** (2143 NE Martin Luther King Jr. Boulevard, Eliot, 503-287-6302, www.queenofsheba.biz) offers up probably the best African food in the city. Fiery stews, mustard greens with flaxseed, and injera bread pulverized with vegetables are but a few of the café's legendary dishes.

SECRET

AFRICAN-AMERICAN

The African-American community is a lively part of the city with many events throughout the year designed to celebrate their heritage and history. "**Juneteenth**" is celebrated with a grand parade and picnic in Alberta Park on the Saturday closest to June 19th. This uniquely African-American holiday commemorates June 19, 1865, when slaves in Texas received word that Lincoln had abolished slavery. In Portland, observation of the holiday was begun in the shipyards in 1944 by Clara Peoples.

SECRET

AFTER HOURS

At the **Sapphire Hotel** (5008 SE Hawthorne Boulevard, 503-232-6333, www.thesapphirehotel.com) you'll get the feeling that you've stumbled into a secret European spot brimming with secrets and spies. A great place for when you are not quite ready to end the evening. Grab a seat at one of the small tables and banquettes or at the bar. Order a bottle of wine, a cocktail, and a bite to eat and expect friendly, welcoming service. It can be very busy on weekends so prepare to join the crush.

Those in the know head to the **Driftwood Room** at the Hotel deLuxe (729 SW 15th Avenue, Downtown, 503-219-2094). Deep, plush, and oozing charm from every pore, it's no wonder they serve concoctions such as the Elizabeth Taylor (crème de violette and champagne). You can almost hear Michael Bublé crooning in the background. And for those late night munchies you can choose from an eclectic menu featuring olives to mac and cheese.

The McMenamins (legendary Portland entrepreneurs) have created **Greater Trumps** (1520 SE 37th Avenue, Hawthorne, 503-235-4530, www.mcmenamins.com), a tiny bar cut into the side of the Bagdad Theater in the Hawthorne district, but this minute bit of real estate appears to have been lifted straight from the streets of Paris. This may be the smallest bar in Portland but its spirit is generous.

When you just have to finish the evening on a high note, take the elevator to the 30th floor for the **Portland City Grill** (111 SW 5th Avenue, Downtown, 503-450-0030, www.portlandcitygrill.com) for some late night feasting or a cocktail. If you're lucky you may even get a window table. Open until midnight from Sunday to Thursday and later on weekend nights.

On Wednesdays, fall through spring, the **Portland Art Museum** (1219 SW Park Avenue, Downtown, 503-226-2811, www.portland artmuseum.org) stays open after regular hours, when it becomes a festive venue where folks can sip wine, enjoy music, dance, and even stroll through the galleries for a more leisurely look.

SECRET
AIRPLANES

To gaze upon one of the largest airplanes ever constructed — and flown — you'll need to travel about 30 miles west of Portland to the

Evergreen Aviation Museum (500 NE Capt. Michael King Smith Way, McMinnville, Oregon, 503-434-4180, www.sprucegoose.org). The museum is home to the *Hughes Flying Boat*, better known as the *Spruce Goose*.

The *Hughes Flying Boat* was built as a personnel and material carrier and was designed to fly across the Atlantic, thus avoiding the World War II German submarines that were sinking Allied ships. Hughes took on the task of building the plane, under government restrictions on using materials critical to the war effort, such as steel and aluminum. Nearly six times bigger than any aircraft of its time, the *Flying Boat* is made of wood.

Skeptics called the aircraft everything from a "flying lumberyard" to the "wooden wonder." It was the press that named it the *Spruce Goose*, a name Hughes despised. What's odd about the nickname is that the plane is constructed of birch, with only small amounts of maple, poplar, balsa, and, yes, spruce.

The *Flying Boat* was not completed until 1947 and has made only one flight. The unannounced decision to fly was made by the pilot, Hughes himself, during a taxi test. The flight stretched only a little over a mile, at an altitude of 70 feet, for about one minute. But the short hop proved to the world that the gigantic machine could indeed fly.

After its famous flight, Hughes stored it in a special hangar out of the public eye for more than 30 years. All that time, Hughes kept the aircraft in ready-to-fly condition. After his death in 1976, it appeared that the plane might be disassembled. The giant plane was saved and moved into a massive hangar near the *Queen Mary* in Long Beach, California. Years later, the plane once again needed a new home. In 1992, the *Hughes Flying Boat* was disassembled and transported by barge up the West Coast, then down the Columbia and Willamette

rivers to Portland. It remained in the Portland area for several months, until the Willamette River's water levels permitted the huge structure to safely pass under the river's many bridges. In 2001, reassembly of the *Hughes Flying Boat* was completed in its new home, the Evergreen Aviation Museum.

SECRET
AL FRESCO

After months of being confined by drizzly, weepy, windy, gray skies, it's no wonder that Portlanders seek the solace of sunshine whenever and wherever possible. That's what makes al fresco dining so popular on days that permit this activity.

Located in an old brick building just a block off Governor Tom McCall Waterfront Park, **A Veritable Quandary** (1220 SW 1st Avenue, Downtown, 503-227-7342, www.veritablequandary.com) has possibly the prettiest patio in town. The chef certainly has a flair for the unusual. You should be prepared for anything from grilled prawns with strawberries and peppercorns to beef skewers with a Peruvian marinade. At the moment "VQ" — so-called by the locals — is hot, hot, hot. For those who want to skip the club scene, it's a good place to be seen.

You want a view of the water but not ready to make a commitment to a full meal? Just beyond River Place is a collection of quick-ish food emporiums with tables on a generously wide sidewalk that include pizza, sushi, and "Mediterranean fusion" ready to take away or take to the sidewalk. Lovely, liberal Portland will even let you take a beer to your sidewalk picnic. During summer months, **Three Degrees** (1510 SW Harbor Way, Downtown, 503-295-6166, www .threedegreesrestaurant.com) offers outdoor seating on the boardwalk with fabulous views of cavorting RiverPlace locals. The tried-and-true Pacific Northwest–bistro fare includes grilled onion-and-beet salad and tender, grilled sirloin steak. For dessert, there's the house-made ice cream in flavors like cinnamon and basil. A nice touch is the constantly changing brews on tap.

The **Compass World Bistro** (4741 SE Hawthorne Boulevard, Mount Tabor, 503-231-4840) has a lovely little garden area complete with fountain, attractive plantings, and a handful of tables. The menu highlights a new cuisine every quarter — sometimes French, Italian, Mediterranean, or American. The food is, quite simply, outstanding. It's thoughtfully prepared and generous in portions. Even if you can't sit outside, the inside is lovely as well.

Typhoon! (2310 NW Everett Street, Northwest, 503-243-7557, and a new location at 410 SW Broadway, 503-224-8285, www .typhoonrestaurants.com) is one of the staples of the "trendy-third" area of town. It's a bit pricey for a Thai restaurant, but on a warm summer night, when the whole front wall slides away for Thai-style open-air dining, you could envision yourself in the Orient. The menu, especially the appetizers, goes beyond standard Thai fare. There's also an extensive tea list.

Bluehour (250 NW 13th Avenue, The Pearl, 503-226-3394, www .bluehouronline.com) is one of Portland's more impressive eateries and has sidewalk patio dining. Nibble on a bruschetta or cheese plate, a dish of olives or dunk into a cheese fondue.

Where better to savor a romantic evening than at **Iorio** (912 SE Haw-thorne Boulevard, Sunnyside, 503-445-4716, www.ioriorestaurant .com). This Italian favorite has a fireplace and a very comfortable atmosphere that puts you in the mood for some fantastic Italian cuisine, among other things.

A cozy setting, a glass of wine, and thou. Well, it's not quite a poem from the *Rubiyat* but **Wine Down** (126 NE 28th Avenue, Northeast, 503-236-9463, www.winedownpdx.com) will certainly put you in poetic mood. This dimly lit, cozy setting is the perfect place to cuddle up with someone and a special vintage. To end the evening, try something from their extensive port menu.

Surprisingly quiet for a city street location, **Bo's Restobar** (400 SW Broadway, Lucia Hotel, Downtown, 503-222-2688, www.boresto bar.com) is a lovely spot for a drink when the sun goes down. If the weather turns sour you can always head into the pocket-size indoor nightclub.

Carafe (200 SW Market Street, Downtown, 503-248-0004, www .carafebistro.com) is an oh-so-French twist on patio dining. Mussels, baguette, pomme frites, and croquet monsieur complete the gastric getaway.

SECRET
ALIENS
❧

You probably won't find aliens in residence at **Things From Another World** (4133 NE Sandy Boulevard, Hollywood, 503-284-4693, www. tfaw.com), but it most likely would be the first place they would come to shop in Portland. Filled with icons of pop culture, sci-fi tomes, comics, toys, games, cards, and graphic novels, it's truly an out-of-this-world experience.

Cosmic Bowling at Grand Central Bowl (808 SE Morrison Street, Mount Tabor, 503-236-BOWL, www.thegrandcentralbowl .com/grand_central) is certainly a place aliens could feel at home, if they enjoyed bowling with disco lights and glow-in-the-dark pins and bowling balls. It's open until quite late in the evening on weekends, for the convenience of local and visiting aliens. Actually, this place's party atmosphere is really a hoot.

SECRET
ALTERNATIVE

The **Hawthorne District**, located in the Mount Tabor neighborhood, is Portland's alternative urban niche. There's a hint of patchouli in the air and wisps of tie-dyed frocks on the inhabitants. The highlight of Hawthorne Boulevard is the historic **Bagdad Theater and Pub** (3702 SE Hawthorne Boulevard, 503-236-9234, www.mcmenamins.com), a wonder of Moorish architecture restored to its original glory by Portland's most popular brewers, the McMenamin brothers. The Bagdad is one of many McMenamin view-and-brew-style venues, where you can watch a recent movie while savoring microbrews and pizza.

This is a lively part of the city. On any given night, live music spills from the open doors of Irish pubs, bibliophiles linger at **Powell's Books**, a branch of the Downtown main store (3723 SE Hawthorne Boulevard, 503-228-4651, www.powells.com), and sidewalk tables host many a disciple of brew, be it beer or coffee. Hawthorne is not exactly the Left Bank of Paris, but it is an agreeable mixture of gentrification and radicalism.

For a taste of Hawthorne, check out such popular haunts as **Thanh Thao**, a tiny restaurant that serves up a large slice of the neighborhood's counterculture atmosphere (4005 SE Hawthorne Boulevard, Mount Tabor, 503-238-6232).

S E C R E T

AMUSEMENTS

Everyone is either a child or a secret child at heart, and we all need amusement parks — particularly small, family-friendly, starter parks. The kind that won't bankrupt you as soon as you walk through the gate. The sort of park that whets your taste for bigger and better.

Oaks Park (7805 SE Oaks Park Way, 503-233-5777, www.oakspark. com), tucked into a grove of old-growth oaks, is a step back to a time when America was innocent, and so was the fun. Built in 1905, this park was where you took the family for a day of rides, midway games, and picnics, and an evening spent dancing in a fairytale pavilion. The Oaks is one of the oldest continuously operating amusement parks in America. Like patrons of other "Trolley Parks" across the country, most of the park's visitors arrived by trolley — in the Oaks' case, cars that ran along the Portland–Oregon City tracks.

Today, you'll find a variety of amusements suitable for almost everyone. Little ones can play on the Frog Hopper, and the brave of heart can opt for the Scream-n-Eagle and Looping Thunder roller coasters.

Speaking of roll — the Oaks Park Skating Rink is part of the complex, and a smoother place to glide away an afternoon or evening would be hard to find. The floor is made of wood and is meticulously maintained. No splinters to fear here!

The historic Oaks Park Dance Pavilion no longer hosts evening dances, but is available for special occasions. The original hardwood floors and carousel animals, now antiques, still decorate the hall. These days it's mostly used for weddings and social occasions, but a hint of the good old days lingers in its ambiance.

Don't forget to take time to see the Oaks Park Museum's displays of days gone by. They tell of the many rides and attractions, like the roller-skating elephant on the midway, the Natatorium, and the Noah's Ark Carousel.

To reach the park, drive west on SE Spokane Street, go over the tracks, and take the first right, then follow the winding road to Oaks Park.

The **Jantzen Beach Amusement Park** on Hayden Island was heralded as Portland's "million-dollar playground" when it opened on May 26, 1928. It was the largest amusement park in the nation, occupying more than 123 acres. There was a carousel, the huge Big Dipper Roller Coaster, midway games, and midget auto racing. The Golden-Canopied Ballroom attracted big-name bands, and people from all over the world came to compete in the dance competitions.

For over four decades, the residents of Portland enjoyed Jantzen Beach Amusement Park. In its later years, the forces of Mother Nature and progress forced the demise of the park, which closed in 1970.

Sadly, all that remains today is the **Jantzen Beach Carousel** (1405 Jantzen Beach Center, 503-286-9103). Legend has it that there is a pair of ghost children in the center of the carousel. Today, the amusements at Jantzen Beach are purely of the shopping variety. But if you need a break, stop by the carousel for a relaxing ride. The outside column of horses will whisk you around at a 10-mph clip.

You'll find **Enchanted Forest** (8462 SE Enchanted Way, Turner, Oregon, 503-371-4242, www.enchantedforest.com) on the road to Salem. This Disney wannabe, with its gentle rides, is especially good for small children.

SECRET

ANGLING

With all the talk about how the salmon are dwindling so rapidly, you might not think it was still possible to fish in Portland. After one trip down the Columbia or Willamette, where you'll see anglers hauling in fat, shiny, sassy fish, you'll start to rethink the picture. Recreational fishing thrives in this city, and although the salmon season is drastically short, you can still haul a 30-pound beauty out of the water. The rest of the year, when salmon fishing is no longer allowed, you'll see fishermen out there trawling for sturgeon, shad, bass, and crappie. Find out what you need to know about licenses from the **Oregon Department of Fish and Wildlife** (503-947-6000, www.dfw.state.or.us).

SECRET

ANTIQUES

Antiques aren't exactly much of a secret anymore, what with reproduction furniture and items of the '70s and '80s being labeled "classic," but you can find your fill of atavistic emporiums in the

Sellwood-Moreland neighborhood. It's similar to other antiquing areas: there's a little of the old and a little of the renovated old. Quaint, almost kitsch, this neighborhood of small Victorian houses is crammed full of antiques, knickknacks, and junque. While there are lots of antiques stores scattered about the city, you won't find a higher concentration anywhere else.

Stars, An Antique Mall (7027 SE Milwaukie Avenue, 503-239-0346, www.starsantique.com) claims to be the largest antiques mall in Portland, and I think it's right. Goods from more than 300 dealers line room after room and row after row of space. If all of that isn't enough just cross the street to a second location they have opened. **Stars and Splendid** (7030 SE Milwaukie Avenue, 503-235-5990) is a lovely addition to the antiques market scene. It's clean, has lots of space between the vendors, and there's lots of help for your questions. **Sellwood Antique Collective** (8027 SE 13th Avenue, Sellwood-Moreland, 503-736-1399) boasts a dizzying array of memorabilia, furniture, lamps, and all sorts of bric-a-brac to tempt your wallet. **The Raven** (7927 SE 13th Avenue, 503-233-8075) specializes in wartime collectibles, such as lead toy soldiers.

Just east of the city, and well worth the trip, is the **Troutdale Antique Mall** (359 E Historic Columbia River Highway, Troutdale, Oregon, 503-674-6820). In fact, all of downtown Troutdale seems to be connected to antiques in one way or another. This slice of nostalgic Americana could have been brought to you by Disney. The city's center strip is clean, well swept, and well lighted, and just oozes "charm." Begin at the far eastern end of E Historic Columbia River Highway (which you will later want to drive, it's so gorgeous). The Troutdale Antiques Mall has two levels of antiques and collectibles that range from china to wooden Indians.

In the market for a life-size metal cow? Or perhaps just a few col-

lectibles and then the opportunity to celebrate your find with a latte or two? **Monticello Antique Marketplace** (8600 SE Stark, Montavilla, 503-256-8600, monticelloantiques.com) is the place for you. It's part upscale antiques, part thrift store finds, and some dealers are better than others. Hidden in the back is a separate book area yielding some unusual finds for those with book lust.

This consortium of more than 60 antique and collectible dealers is a true treasure chest. Its items are clean, displayed in a customer-friendly fashion, it is handicapped accessible, and it is even air-conditioned for those occasional humid days.

Take time from your treasure hunt to stop for sustenance at the **Troutdale General Store** (289 E Historic Columbia River Highway, 503-492-7912), a turn-of-the-century-style soda fountain and café. The menu is limited to soups, sandwiches, and a daily special, so turn your appetite to a fountain specialty, such as a root beer float.

You'll find "old stuff" even in the heart of downtown Portland. An area currently experiencing massive gentrification is The Pearl. Bordered by the Willamette River to the north, NW Broadway to the east, West Burnside Street to the south, and the I-405 Freeway to the west, it is filled with antiquing surprises. **Thea's Interiors** (1204 NW Glisan Street, The Pearl, 503-274-0275, www.theasinteriors.com) carries antiques and collectibles with a European twist. Thea can also help you with home staging and interior updating.

Finally, there's the **Old Town Chinatown Antique Market** (32 NW 1st Avenue), adjacent to the Saturday Market. On market day weekends from March through December there's a hefty crowd, but on a weekday in January you may well have the place to yourself. With more than 20 dealers on hand, there's no telling what you may discover. You might find a heavy, carved sideboard, an unusual piece of

Franciscan "El Patio," or maybe even your auntie's mink tails. If you want to save yourself parking headaches, take the MAX train. It stops just a few feet from the market.

SECRET

ARCHITECTURE

Portland is better known for the lattice of bridges spanning its two rivers and for its evergreen ambiance than for its architecture. However, over the years, it has amassed a unique and distinctly Northwest Coast style.

In the early 1970s, Portland was just beginning its era of urban gentrification. Seedy waterfront buildings were being renovated into river walks, trendy bistros, and boutiques. As the economy improved, so did the downtown landscape. In fact, because Portland has clung so tenaciously to its past, the city has a much more European look than you would expect.

The Old Church (1422 SW 11th Avenue, Downtown, 503-222-2031, www.oldchurch.org), built in 1883, is one of the oldest and most beautiful buildings in the Pacific Northwest. A striking example of Carpenter Gothic, the church hosted both Presbyterian and Baptist congregations (not at the same time) until 1967. Its ornate window traceries, archways, and buttresses meld agreeably with chimney spires and a porte-cochere. No longer a home to any one congregation, the Old Church is now a non-profit historic site. Every Wednesday, the Old Church Society presents free sack-lunch concerts in the 350-seat auditorium.

And then there are Portland's grand buildings. **City Hall** (1221 SW 4th Avenue, Downtown, 503-823-4000), built in 1895 and restored in 1998, is one of the grandest buildings in the city. The $30-million restoration program managed to return most of the original charm to the structure, much of which had been destroyed by haphazard changes over its lifetime (like a series of bad haircuts). The City Council's chambers have been returned to their original layout. There, wood paneling has been removed from the main-floor windows, allowing natural light to flow into the legislative chamber. The building sports Italian marble throughout and a lot of decorative copper plating.

Just wandering the downtown area you'll come upon some remarkable buildings that have stood the test of time. The **Bishop's House** (3rd Avenue and Stark Street, Downtown), constructed in 1879, was originally living quarters for Catholic Archbishop François Blanchet. Since then, the Bishop's House has been home to a speakeasy, the Ramsay Sign Company, and an architectural firm. Currently, it's the site of a Lebanese restaurant.

The **Dekum Building** (3rd Avenue and Washington Street, Downtown) is a fine example of Romanesque architecture, constructed entirely out of materials native to Oregon. Look for the carved sandstone on the first three stories and local red brick on the top five floors. At the time of construction, the floral terra-cotta friezes represented a unique departure from the cast-iron architecture of the day.

A short walk down 3rd Avenue will bring you to the heart of the **Yamhill Historic District**. During the mid-1880s, this area was the focus of commercial trade and a vibrant public market. Shop owners at the time constructed elaborate cast-iron storefronts. Today, many of those stores are now restaurants, galleries, and specialty boutiques. All are protected on the National Register of Historic Places.

From 3rd Avenue, walk west along Yamhill Street until you come to Park Avenue and the beginning of the **Park Blocks.** The blocks are noted for having perhaps the oldest and largest remaining stand of elm trees in the county. The South Park Blocks are lined with elegant churches and public buildings. Flanking the southern end of the Park Blocks is Portland State University, home to some 16,000 students.

The **Multnomah County Central Library** (801 sw 10th Avenue, at Yamhill Street, Downtown, 503-988-5123, www.multcolib.org) was built in 1913 by noted architect A.E. Doyle and extensively renovated in 1997. This impressive edifice houses more than 17 miles of bookshelves and the delightful Beverly Cleary Children's Library.

The oldest remaining public building in the Northwest is **Pioneer Courthouse** (sw Broadway and sw Morrison Street, Downtown), built in 1869. This Palladian structure features an octagonal cupola. It currently houses a post office and a United States Court of Appeals.

Not all of Portland's notable architecture harkens to the 19th century. **Pioneer Place** (700 sw 5th Avenue, Downtown, 503-228-5800, www.pioneerplace.com) features a soaring glass-topped rotunda. The **Portland Building** (5th Avenue and Madison Street, Downtown), completed in 1982, was the first major postmodern structure in the United States. This whimsical office tower was designed to represent the Northwest with an American Indian motif, making extensive use of turquoise and earth tones. Above the front entrance to the building kneels Raymond Kaskey's *Portlandia*, the second-largest hammered-copper statue in the world (see "Secret Copper"). For a nearly eye-level view of the sculpture, take the escalator at the front of the Standard Insurance Plaza building up to the landing. Awesome.

S E C R E T

A R T

Fountains dance, sidewalks talk, and weathervanes trumpet. Public art abounds in this city. Why? It's due in part to the generosity of the citizens and in part to a program that requires all new large-scale commercial and public building projects to include public art in the budget. Every City of Portland office building proudly displays its signature mural, sculpture, painting, relief, or fountain.

After all, this is the city where Mayor Bud Clark decreed that you should "expose yourself to art" and had the courage — and the trench coat — to pose for what is now a notorious poster of him flashing a statue of a nude woman. If you'd like to re-create your own version of that infamous work, you'll find the statue, *Kvinneakt*, on the Transit Mall, near the northeast corner of sw 5th Avenue and sw Washington Street (Downtown).

Portland's public art has great whimsy and depth. You'll find bits in the most unexpected places. For example, a bronze elk is set in a fountain on sw Main Street between sw 3rd and 4th avenues (Downtown) that once served as a watering trough for both horses and humans. The fountain is still the primary watering hole for Portland's mounted patrol. And it's probably the most pleasing traffic divider anywhere.

On sw Yamhill and sw Morrison streets (Downtown), look for the playful bronze bears, beavers, ducks, and deer wandering down the sidewalk and playing in the small pools of water.

For a different perspective on Portland's public art program, ride the MAX train to the **Oregon Convention Center** (777 NE Martin Luther King Jr. Boulevard, 503-235-7575) to see one of the state's most impressive art collections. It includes works by local artists, as well as pieces from around the world. Of particular note is *Principia*, a pendulum hanging in the center's north tower above a 30-foot halo of suspended rays and a circular blue terrazzo floor inlaid with brass and stones.

Even the transit system has participated in the public art program. One of my favorite pieces is at the **Gresham Central Transit Center** (350 NE 8th Avenue). A living room setting, complete with a TV, has been constructed out of concrete. It is so realistic that the first time I saw it, I was convinced someone had left his furniture behind. For more about art on the MAX, see "Secret Transit Stops."

Even the bus system joins in the act with ART, the Cultural Bus (see "Secret Bus Routes").

S E C R E T

AUTOMOBILES

For those who drool over swept-back fins, boat-tail beauties, and barrel backs, the **Forest Grove Concours d'Elegance** (Pacific University campus, Forest Grove, Oregon, 503-357-3006, www .forestgroveconcours.org) is the place to indulge those fantasies. The event, usually held in late July, celebrates the auto in almost every way imaginable. Enthusiasts bring more than 300 antique, collector, and specialty cars together for both display and judging. The tree-shaded glade on the Pacific University campus provides a unique setting for walking among the cars.

SECRET B&Bs

Bed and breakfasts share a reputation for being cozy, warm, and congenial. To my way of thinking, a B&B is where you go for R&R: rest and recuperation, or romance and rest, or romance and romance.

The **Heron Haus** (2545 NW Westover Road, Hillside, 503-274-1846, www.heronhaus.com) is filled with cushy furnishings, snuggly quilts, and the aroma of freshly baked pastries. This English Tudor home in the heart of Portland's northwest hills features a solarium, a pool, and six spacious, sun-filled suites. All of them have a Hawaiian theme and name. Be sure to ask for the Ko Suite. Once you've tried the shower with seven nozzles, you may never be able to shower at home again.

Even from afar, there is something special about the elegant Queen Anne home that houses **The Lion and the Rose** (1810 NE 15th Avenue, Irvington, 503-287-9245 or 800-955-1647, www.lionrose.com). From the lofty cupola and turrets to the grand portico, this is a classic Victorian bed and breakfast. The spacious rooms are decorated with historically accurate furnishings. The bathrooms can best be described as snug, but that's a small inconvenience.

Portland's **White House** (1914 NE 22nd Avenue, Irvington, 503-287-7131 or 800-272-7131, www.portlandswhitehouse.com) bears a remarkable resemblance to its DC namesake. There is a circular driveway, and both an east and west wing. This residence is very popular with wedding parties, so weekends can sometimes be a bit frantic. But the home is gracious and elegant, with bedrooms scrupulously maintained. To top it off, breakfast is a three-course adventure.

S E C R E T

BACKYARD

Not every city is fortunate enough to have a hiking/picnicking/ snowboarding/skiing mountain in its backyard. But that's what **Mount Hood** is to Portland. Mount Hood is second only to Mount Fuji in Japan as one of the most-climbed mountains in the world. At 11,235 feet, it's Oregon's highest peak. This popular playground offers five wilderness areas, an excellent trail system, fishing, camping, and skiing.

There are three well-known areas for skiing on the mountain: Timberline, Skibowl, and Mount Hood Meadows. Timberline is the only place in North America that offers summer skiing.

According to a Native American legend, Mount Hood was a brave warrior named Wy'east who fell in love with Mount St. Helens, a beautiful Indian maiden. Wy'east vied for the maiden's attentions with Mount Adams, his rival. Unable to decide between the two braves, Mount St. Helens would occasionally erupt out of frustration. Hmmm, I wonder what those two braves did to set her off in 1980?

While at the mountain, be sure to check out Timberline Lodge, an impressive stone-and-timber structure built as a Works Progress Administration project in 1937. The hotel is still open to visitors and is one of the finest hotels in the state. Does it look eerily familiar? That's because Timberline Lodge was the exterior setting for the 1980 film version of Stephen King's *The Shining*.

A favorite route to the mountain is via the Columbia River Gorge. At the beginning of the 20th century, the Columbia River Highway was first envisioned: a road stretching from Troutdale to The Dalles that

would wind past some of the most awe-inspiring views imaginable. Take exit 17 from I-84 to get to the Scenic Columbia River Highway. The highway curves and sways its way past a ribbon of river, through lush green foliage, and alongside alternately gently flowing and swiftly raging waterfalls. And, just when you think it can't possibly get any prettier, you reach the top. At 725 feet above the Columbia River, the Vista House at Crown Point offers a sweeping view of the Columbia Gorge, stretching out over 30 miles. You'll need to rejoin I-84 to arrive at Mount Hood, but this detour is well worth the effort.

SECRET

BALLET

It's no surprise that a city the size of Portland has a ballet company. What is a surprise is that it rehearses outdoors, in a tent in the South Park Blocks, during the annual **Oregon Ballet Theatre Exposed!** festival. Spectators are free to fill the tent's chairs at lunchtime and nosh on goodies from brown bags. So, how good is the company indoors? When the **Oregon Ballet Theatre** (818 SE 6th Avenue, 503-222-5538, www.obt.org) toured New York City, it wowed audiences with its strong blend of classical and modern ballet danced by an energetic young company. Director James Canfield concentrates on his own choreography and that of visiting artists; he supplements new pieces with reworkings of American classics by the likes of DeMille, Robbins, and Balanchine.

SECRET

BALLROOMS

"I know a place where the music is fine and the lights are always low. I know a place where we can go." **The Crystal Ballroom** (1332 W Burnside Street, Downtown, 503-225-0047, www.mcmenamins.com) could have launched itself straight from the lyrics of the Petula Clark song. This is the place to dance and listen. The "floating" dance floor may make you feel like you're dancing on a rolling ship when the crowd is large, but for cheek-to-cheek twosomes, it's like floating on air. Almost everything goes on here — ballroom dancing, complete with lessons; alternative rock shows; and concerts by neo-hippie bands. There's literally something for everyone. The ballroom is open only during scheduled events.

Should seductive salsa be more your style, head for **Andrea's Cha Cha Club** (832 SE Grand Avenue, Buckman, 503-230-1166). The wood-paneled basement of the Grand Café is Grand Central for Latin dancing in the city. Lessons are available for the timid, but the bold can go ahead and jump right into the action.

Housed in a 1907 former Masonic Lodge, **The Secret Society** (116 NE Russell Street, Eliot, 503-493-3600, www.secretsociety.net) is a jewel waiting to be discovered. Take one part speakeasy cocktail lounge, one part classic ballroom, and one part well-hidden recording studio. Mix well and enjoy! The Secret Society Lounge is open nightly, featuring classic pre-prohibition cocktails, real absinthe, and delicious local wine and beer. Food and drink specials daily, with late night happy hour from 10 PM to close.

SECRET

BARGE

"Sweet Mary," the proprietor of a brothel, is one of the city's more notorious historical figures. In the late 1800s, Mary operated her bordello on a barge that ran up and down the Willamette River. Technically, she was outside of everyone's jurisdiction.

SECRET

BARNYARD

Pasturelands once stretched west of Portland between Hillsdale and Beaverton. Due to population growth and commercial production, times have changed. **Alpenrose Dairy** (6149 sw Shattuck Road, Beaverton, Oregon, 503-244-1133, www.alpenrose.com) stands as a reminder of quieter days. In this once-thriving dairy community, Alpenrose is the only survivor, and it has developed into much, much more than a dairy. Among other attractions, it's got a baseball stadium, where games have been played since 1956.

Not far from the stadium is Dairyville, a replica of a western frontier town. There are dozens of false-front shops, which are filled with treasured antiques. There's also a doll museum, a harness store, a music shop, and even an old-fashioned ice cream parlor. Behind Dairyville, you'll discover the Quarter-Midget Racing Arena and the Circuit d'Alpenrose velodrome.

There isn't a holiday you couldn't spend at the dairy. At Christmastime, a make-believe, snow-covered Storybook Lane is filled with nursery-rhyme characters, such as the Three Little Pigs and Peter Rabbit. The residents of the lane's holiday cottages are piglets, bunnies, and goats, part of the menagerie of farm animals that Dairyland keeps on hand to delight children year-round. At Easter, there's the annual Egg Hunt, and summer is the time for the Li'l Britches Rodeo.

Duyck's Peachy-Pig Farm (34840 sw Johnson School Road, Cornelius, Oregon, 503-357-3570, www.peachypigfarm.com) is the place to head for the freshest fruits and vegetables in summer and fall. Pick them yourself, or let staffers pick them for you. Gather enough for an impromptu picnic and gorge yourself on local blackberries, marionberries, rhubarb, walnuts, and grapes.

S E C R E T
B A Z A A R
꘎

The well-named **Bazaar of the Bizarre** (7202 NE Glisan Street, Center, 503-235-3552) stocks a truly unusual inventory of tidbits, most with a gruesome factor. There are lots of things that glow in the dark, hard-to-find toys, and an astonishing array of anatomically correct reproductions of hearts, brains, and eyeballs — maybe because it's so close to the Providence Medical Center?

Cargo (380 NW 13th Avenue, The Pearl, 503-209-8349, www.cargoinc.com) is two floors filled with lots of oriental "stuff." From simple decorations to intricately carved oriental armoires, books to magic tricks, paper lanterns to jewelry, this is a fun stop. You won't have any difficulty locating this store, as strings of paper lanterns and decorations hang jauntily from the roof around three sides of the building — very eye-catching.

SECRET

BEACHES

For a city with two rivers, Portland has surprisingly few beaches, mostly because not everyone wants to swim in the Columbia with all that river traffic. But there are beaches to be found. On a warm weekend, head to **Rooster Rock State Park** (take I-84 east to exit 25, 503-986-0707 or 800-551-6949). But be sure to get there early, because all 1,800 parking spaces along this strip of sandy beach have been known to fill up. There's a logged-off swimming hole in the Columbia River, a boat launch, and docks for anglers. At the far eastern end, a separate beach has been designated "clothing optional" — how Euro-trash!

Sauvie Island (Route 30, west of Portland to the Sauvie Island Bridge) also has long sandy beaches on which to while away the day. It's a short 15-minute drive to the island from downtown. And aside from soaking up the sun, you can go berry picking, frog hunting, and picnicking. There is only one road onto the island, so be prepared for a traffic jam on warm summer days.

If what you want is a real beach — miles of sand, waves rolling into the shore, and a good stiff breeze — you'll need to plan a day trip to the Oregon coast. You really should, anyway. There is a wild remoteness to the shoreline, unfettered by any barrier reefs.

Cannon Beach (75 miles from Portland), the closest ocean beach to the city, is a great place to fly a kite, ride a horse, play in the water, or simply daydream on the sand. The water is cold most of the time, but on really hot days it will warm up — a little. The town of Cannon Beach is loaded with boutiques, galleries, bookshops, eateries, and small hotels.

SECRET

BIFFYS

Isn't that what you call the bathroom? Restroom? Loo? Well, when you have to go, you have to go. The most central public restrooms are those in Pioneer Courthouse Square (Downtown), near the TriMet Office. The lobby opens at 8:30 AM and closes at 5 PM. On weekends, the hours vary. Further south, there are public restrooms in the Clay Street parking garage (Downtown), but I don't really recommend them. You can also find restrooms in Pioneer Place, Macy's, and Nordstrom (all Downtown).

SECRET

BIRTHDAY

April 6 is Portland's birthday. Doesn't every city have one?

SECRET

BOATS

Don't have time for a sentimental journey? You need a jetboat! **Willamette Jetboat Excursions** (1945 SE Water Avenue, Downtown, 503-231-1532 or 888-538-2628, www.willamettejet.com), which moors its craft at the OMSI dock, plies the Willamette from the northern dry docks all the way south to Willamette Falls, where you'll get an up-close-and-personal view. Just a note of advice — be prepared to get wet. Very wet. Especially in the front row. These lightning-fast, open-air speedboats can do some amazing turns and circles, and are just the ticket for a quick tour of the Willamette River.

Or maybe you'd like to add some special delivery to your river journey? **Mail Boat Hydro Jets** (Gold Beach, Oregon, 541-247-7033 or 800-458-3511, www.mailboat.com) still make the original 64-mile mail run along the Rogue River through Copper Canyon. It's a fantastic way to see deer, otter, and bear along the riverbanks as eagles and ospreys swoop overhead. Trips of several lengths are available. Most include a stop, during which you can buy a meal. If you're taking this trip, be prepared for some long uphill hikes to the comfort stations.

Want to pretend you're setting out on a sunset cruise from the harbor of Monte Carlo, with nothing ahead of you but an evening of dining and music, and a beautiful skyline? Come aboard the ***Portland Spirit***, ***Willamette Star***, or ***Crystal Dolphin*** (110 SE Caruthers Street, Hosford-Abernethy, 503-224-3900 or 800-224-3901, www .portlandspirit.com) for a special treat. It's the Pacific Northwest rather than the Riviera, but Portland's downtown skyline is very impressive in its own right. The largest of the yachts, the *Portland Spirit*, is a favorite with locals. They sail to celebrate anniversaries, birthdays, and visiting relatives. As well as sunset cruises, there are also lunch cruises, brunch cruises, Friday escape cruises, club dance cruises, dinner theater cruises, fireworks cruises, and just plain-vanilla sightseeing cruises.

For a gentler glide down the river, try the *Columbia Gorge*, now operated by the folks at Portland Spirit, or the *Rose* (1945 SE Water Avenue, Portland, 503-286-7673, www.sternwheelerrose.com). There is something simultaneously historic and romantic about traveling on a sternwheeler. It's so easy to imagine that you are an early pioneer, seeing the incredible beauty of the Columbia River gliding past you. The ships operate most weekends and evenings.

Not all boating activities happen on the Willamette or Columbia Rivers. The Sandy River originates on the slopes of Mt. Hood, and winds it way some 50 miles to join the Columbia River. This gently flowing river runs through many beautiful areas and is ideal for boating. **River Trails** (336 E Historic Columbia River Highway, Troutdale, 503-667-1964, www.rivertrailstroutdale.com) rents kayaks for serious adventurers. It can also rent a rubber tube, float, and life preserver to those who want a leisurely drift down the river. The staff at River Trails are ready to lend advice on where to enter and exit the river safely.

SECRET
BOHO

Outside of San Francisco and New York, Portland is one of the last strongholds of Bohemian culture. Although up to the minute in many respects, Portlanders take a healthy, retro, counterculture look at the world. And many do it from the tables in a collection of cafés worthy of Allen Ginsberg.

The Cricket Café (3159 SE Belmont Street, Sunnyside, 503-235-9348) is funky, hip, and affordable. The strong points that draw in all comers, from yuppie families to boho singles, include cornbread biscuits to die for and a soothing blend of both vegan and meathead dishes.

The **Café Lena** (2239 SE Hawthorne Boulevard, Sunnyside, 503-238-7087) is an art-filled den cluttered with poets and those who yearn to take pen in hand. Once you find a table, it's yours for as long as you like — or at least until inspiration strikes. Soft acoustic guitar music strums in the background, just low enough to allow eavesdropping on a nearby anarchistic conversation. The espresso is good and the house coffee fine enough to keep you drinking refills.

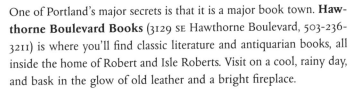

SECRET
BOOKS

One of Portland's major secrets is that it is a major book town. **Hawthorne Boulevard Books** (3129 SE Hawthorne Boulevard, 503-236-3211) is where you'll find classic literature and antiquarian books, all inside the home of Robert and Isle Roberts. Visit on a cool, rainy day, and bask in the glow of old leather and a bright fireplace.

There are numerous chain stores, small emporiums devoted to a single genre, and the granddaddy bookstore of them all — **Powell's City of Books**, occupying an entire municipal block (1005 W Burnside Street, The Pearl, 503-228-4651). Bibliophiles have been known to expire from sheer happiness or exhaustion at Powell's. Prepare to spend hours — no, days — within these walls. The store offers not only up-to-the-minute releases, but also out-of-date, out-of-print, and collectible books. The store is color coded, and an easy-to-follow map will guide you to the section you desire. Each section of the store is staffed by helpful and knowledgeable sales folks. After all, this is book nirvana! And don't forget to ride the elevator. It has three doors. Think about that one for a while.

Aside from the main Powell's location, you can also satisfy your need for tomes at one of its specialty shops, including **Powell's Technical Bookstore** (33 NW Park Avenue, The Pearl, 503-228-4651). You'll even find two outlets at the Portland International Airport.

The lovely thing about independent bookstores like **Murder by the Book** (3210 SE Hawthorne Boulevard, 503-232-9995, www.mbtb.com) is their ability to specialize. MBTB has an extensive selection of mysteries; thrillers; suspense, detective, and crime books; and any other genre you can imagine that will give you a sleepless night. MBTB is the location you want for special orders of hard-to-get, sometimes out-of-print publications. There's no mystery in the fact that MBTB is murder incorporated — you can find videos, puzzles, dinner-party games, pins, and other mystery miscellany within these walls.

Periodicals and Book Paradise (1928 NE 42nd Avenue, 503-234-6003) — two stores under one roof — stocks almost a million magazines. Issues published within the past year sell for 75 percent off the cover price. On the book side, you'll find everything from mysteries to computers, art to health. Book Paradise doesn't specialize — it just offers a good overall selection.

Does reading cookbooks make you hungry? Still in Sunnyside,

Powell's Books for Cooks and Gardeners (3747 SE Hawthorne Boulevard, 503-235-3802) is perfectly located next door to a trendy grocery called Pastaworks. The Powell's shop is delightful. Cookbooks reign supreme, and it's a favorite stop on the book-signing circuit for noted cookbook authors. There's also an excellent selection of cooking gear, colorful dishes, and table linens. And oh, yes, you will also find gardening books and a gardening section, complete with pots and wind chimes.

A radical holdout for the counterculture is **Laughing Horse Books** (12 NE 10th Avenue, 503-236-2893). And a gold mine for used and rare titles, with almost 30,000 at last count, is **Paper Moon Books** (4707 SE Belmont Street, Sunnyside, 503-239-8848).

Got time for a lovely, long, book-browsing walk? Try the Sunnyside neighborhood, where you'll find a miracle mile and a half filled with volumes. Stores include **In Other Words** (8 B NE Killingsworth Street, 503-232-6003, www.inotherwords.org), where all the books are written by women. This non-profit bookstore provides readers with feminist, gay/lesbian, and holistic works not available at mainstream venues. There's also a good selection of children's books.

Have you ever wondered where old library books end up? **Title Wave Bookstore** (216 NE Knott Street, Eliot, 503-988-5021) is the place to find more than 20,000 volumes culled from libraries around the city. The books sell for bargain prices, even old encyclopedia sets. And how are the books arranged? Dedicated volunteers keep them all in order by the Dewey decimal system, of course! Aside from books, there are also magazines, CDs, videos, and audio books.

SECRET

BREAKFASTS

CHOW (505 NW 14th Avenue, The Pearl, 503-274-2469, www
.cafechow.com) is literally the place to fill up your tummy with
breakfast. This former gasoline station has been transformed into a
bright and kitchsy breakfast and lunch emporium. Menu favorites
include an egg, cream cheese, and smoked salmon scramble, and a
special house-made granola.

Bertie Lou's (8051 SE 17th Avenue, Sellwood-Moreland, 503-239-
1177) has been a Portland breakfast destination for decades. This
is a terrific place to carb up before going on an antique trek in the
historic Sellwood-Moreland district.

If you're willing to travel a little out of town, or if you've been sav-
ing money on a hotel by staying outside the city, then you'll be in
the right neighborhood to try one of the following restaurants. Both
are in Greshman, but don't let that stop you: Gresham is on the way
to Mount Hood.

Heidi's of Gresham (1230 NE Cleveland Avenue, 503-667-4200
www.heidisofgresham.com) tries its best to be either Swiss or German in décor and wait-staff dress, but it doesn't succeed (dirndls really
don't look good on people over 40). And that's okay, because the
food really sings. In fact, it yodels. The omelettes are to die for — big,
fluffy, and filled with an almost endless variety of combinations. The
lunches and dinners aren't bad either. Attached to the restaurant is
a gift shop with a quite good selection of trinkets, including items
made out of the ash from the Mount St. Helens explosion back in
1980.

Elmer's Pancake & Steak House (1590 NE Burnside Road, Gresham, Oregon, 503-665-5144, www.elmers-restaurants.com) is also high on my list of breakfast eateries. The pancakes and omelette platters are generous, the wait staff is courteous, and the prices are reasonable.

SECRET
BREWS
❦

If you can visit Portland without a stop at one of its many microbreweries, well, you simply don't like beer. But if you do, you may well go blissfully crazy attempting to try them all in a single visit. For more than a decade, Portland has been known as the epicenter of America's craft-brewing renaissance. Beer writer Fred Eckhardt has argued that Portland is the greatest beer town on earth. Okay, we admit that Mr. Eckhardt resides in Portland, but where else would you expect a dedicated beer connoisseur to live? Portland, after all, boasts more microbreweries, brewpubs, and outlets (pubs offering microbrews on tap) per capita than any other American city.

Let's say you've only tasted beer from a can. Where do you begin to sample the vast selection available? Ask for help. Portlanders love to talk about beer. Watch the skies — the darker the skies, the darker the beer in your glass. Winter is the perfect time to soothe your thirst with a pint of stout, porter, or bock. Beware the buzz factor. Microbrews do tend to be stronger than the average mass-produced beer.

Wait a minute! Before you begin a tasting spree, you'd better have a good idea of what's out there. Here's a little cheat sheet, so you won't sound as though all you've ever had to drink is Budweiser.

Golden ale — This light summer ale is usually available in late spring.

Pale ale — A more bitter or hoppy variety of ale, this beer has a higher alcohol content than others in its class.

Extra special bitter — A summertime favorite, this brew packs a hoppy finish.

India pale ale — Named after the variety first brewed for the British stationed in India, this is a favorite warm-weather beer.

Brown ale — It's full in body and sweeter than other ales.

Scottish ale — Malty Scottish ale frequently has a smoky finish.

Wheat beer — This cloudy, unfiltered brew is served with a lemon wedge.

Porter — This is a dark, heavy ale for a winter's day.

Stout — It's as dark as night, with a hop-flavored finish.

Winter ales — These ales are heavy in taste and alcohol content.

Barley wine — This is truly an acquired taste, with twice the alcohol content of ale.

July is a wonderful time to begin your sampling sally. Oregon's brewers take their taps to tents along Portland's waterfront for the **Oregon Brewers Festival** (www.oregonbrewfest.com). You'll be in good company, as this annual event attracts nearly 80,000 brew enthusiasts. If you can't wait or won't be in town for the festival, here are a few other places to try.

Start with the **Horse Brass Pub** (4534 SE Belmont Street, Sunnyside, 503-232-2202, www.horsebrass.com), which serves up fine British and German beers in an authentic pub atmosphere. This establishment inspired many a brewer, and today it serves as a showplace for the best of both local brews and European imports.

The BridgePort Brewing Company (1318 NW Northrup Street,

503-241-7179, www.bridgeportbrew.com) is Portland's oldest operating microbrewery. You'll find it in the heart of the Pearl District in a renovated rope factory. BridgePort Nutbrown Ale, known as "the original," is served only in this location. You can also try Blue Heron Pale Ale, known as BridgePort Pale Ale outside the Northwest. Take the time for a tour of the dark recesses of this magnificent building. The timbers and floors are still soaked with oils from the original rope factory. In true pub fashion, there's good pub grub, including focaccia, sausage sandwiches, and pizzas made with crust from unfermented beer wort.

The Pilsner Room, adjacent to **McCormick and Schmick's Harborside Restaurant** (309 sw Montgomery Street, RiverPlace Marina, Downtown, 503-220-1865, www.mccormickandschmicks. com), is the home of Full Sail Ale. This restaurant/brewery is part of RiverPlace Marina, a posh collection of shops, galleries, and condos between downtown Portland and the Willamette River. If you like your hops with a yuppie flair, this is the place to sip.

Should your palate pine for a more gourmet brew, head for the **Hair of the Dog Brewing Company** (4509 SE 23rd Avenue, Sunnyside, 503-232-6585, www.hairofthedog.com). Located in a somewhat dilapidated warehouse in industrial southeast Portland (be brave!), this unpretentious locale produces beers on a par with some of the best German and Belgian brews. There's no food, no entertainment, and no smoking — just a good brewery tour and a chance to sample some high-octane beer.

Prepare to stand in line to belly up to the bar at the **Lucky Labrador Brewing Company** (915 SE Hawthorne Boulevard, Buckman, 503-236-3555, www.luckylab.com). This sparse and somewhat dark pub becomes standing room only on weekends. On a cool wintry day, try the Black Lab Stout, with its rich flavor and ample hops. This is the least flashy or upscale of Portland's many brewpubs, but its well-crafted ales and unpretentious atmosphere will make you a devotee in rapid time. The food is limited, but a local version of a bento box (chicken or veggie, barbecued on an outdoor grill) complements many of the brews.

The two-mile drive down narrow and sometimes picturesque Multnomah Boulevard in the Garden Home neighborhood to the **Old Market Pub and Brewery** (6959 sw Multnomah Boulevard, 503-BIG-BEER, www.drinkbeerhere.com) will make you forget that the bustling downtown area is but a few minutes away. The brewery produces a range of ales, including a light pale ale, the hop-heavy Dr. Dan's Backward Bitter, and a rather dry stout. To give your taste buds a tingle, sample the jalapeño-spiced pale ale, if it's available. The pub itself has a market theme highlighted by giant murals of fruit labels and hanging scales that now serve as planters. The menu is almost as large as the building with many varieties of calzones, nacho platters, burgers, and pizzas.

If you are looking for a *biergarten* nirvana, you will find it on the road to Troutdale at **McMenamins Edgefield Brewery** (2126 sw Halsey Street, Troutdale, 503-669-8610 or 800-669-8610). Edgefield is a brewery, winery, pub, movie theater, upscale restaurant, and bed and breakfast — all within the confines of a restored 1911 county poor farm. To experience Edgefield to the fullest, it is best to stay overnight in one of the 100 B&B rooms. This will allow you plenty of time to take a peek at the brewery, which produces Black Rabbit Porter, Bagdad Golden, and Terminator Stout; munch on burgers and fries in the pub; take in a movie; and finish off the day with a meal in the Black Rabbit Restaurant.

SECRET

BRITISH

Portland has a soft spot for things anglo, mostly the tea (see "Secret Tea"). But, sometimes, you need a stronger brew. You'll find that at the **Moon and Sixpence British Pub** (2014 NE 42nd Avenue, Hollywood, 503-288-7802). Boddington's Cream Ale, Guinness, and taps of Tetley's Bitter are just a few of the beers among the seemingly endless options. Owner Kevin Dorney is happy to offer advice to the novice. The atmosphere here will almost make you believe you've taken a trip back to jolly old England. The owners didn't just hang out a few flags and put a red telephone booth in the loo. No, this is authentic stuff, including oak benches (after a few drinks they get more comfortable) and a menu complete with Mum's Bread Pudding.

SECRET

BROTHERS

The McMenamin brothers, Mike and Brian, have turned a single restaurant and pub (Produce Row, now under different ownership) into a funky beer and burger empire stretching all the way to Seattle. In 1985, the brothers began brewing their own beer at the Hillsdale Pub and Brewery, to serve onsite and to supply other McMenamin restaurants in the area. Their enterprise has been nothing short of phenomenal. But this is no ordinary chain. In fact, you can't really call it a chain, because all the establishments are so different from each other. The brothers have converted aging theaters, ballrooms, and even a county home for the poor into some of the most unusual eateries and entertainment venues Portland has to offer.

Their flair for innovation is legendary in the city. And why shouldn't it be? The McMenamin brothers now own more than 30 establishments. What you'll come to enjoy about these places is that they are typically Portland: laid-back, cool, and filled with some good Northwest art.

SECRET
BUS ROUTES

The cheapest — okay, most cost-effective — way to view the sights of Portland is via the bus or MAX train. ART, **the Cultural Bus** (secretly known as Bus #63), takes an impressive cultural route through the city, stopping at or near such venues as the International Rose Test Garden, the Oregon History Center, the Oregon Museum of Science and Industry (OMSI), the Portland Art Museum, the Portland Center for the Performing Arts, Governor Tom McCall Waterfront Park, the Oregon Zoo, the World Forestry Center Museum, the Vietnam Veterans Living Memorial, the Japanese Garden, Memorial Coliseum, and the Oregon Convention Center. Wow! You get all that for just the price of a bus ticket. If you want to hop on and off all day and see everything, buy a day pass for just $4.75. For more information on this route and others, contact TriMet, Portland's transit company (503-238-RIDE, www.trimet.org).

SECRET

BUTTONS AND BOWS
❧

Need a little frippery in your life? The **Button Emporium and Ribbonry** (1016 sw Taylor Street, Downtown, 503-228-6372, www .buttonemporium.com) is awash in French lace, exquisite ribbons, ribbon embroidery supplies, gorgeous buttons, and Australian magazines. Australian magazines? If you want luscious patterns to create heirloom clothing for children and adults, those in the know say the Australians appear to have cornered the market on smocking, pleating, and generally complex patterns.

SECRET

CAFÉS
❧

Want a really good café? And, a place you can take a vegan to brunch, your sweetie for a romantic outing, or be comfortable on your own? Head to **The Farm Café** (10 SE 7th Avenue, Eastside, 503-736-FARM, www.thefarmcafe.com). The food is great but the wait can be long. On special occasions such as Valentine's Day or any weekend morning the crowd starts to line up early. What's all the fuss about? Terrific cheesecake, housemade hummus, herb-crusted tofu, and gnocchi with sweet potato, just to name a few items.

Paragon (1309 NW Hoyt Street, The Pearl, 503-833-5060, www .paragonrestaurant.com) has been the "neighborhood" gathering spot in the Pearl since it opened almost 12 years ago. The burgers are more than ample in size and the French fries, cooked in rosemary-scented oil, will keep you coming back. There's a "Pearl" vibe to this place, it's more than just your average café — it's sleek, chic, and definitely artistic.

Papa Haydn (5829 SE Milwaukie Avenue, Sellwood-Moreland, 503-232-9440, www.papahaydn.com) has a casual "Reedy" (Reed College) atmosphere and world-class desserts. People line up for these calories — not just out the door, but also away down the block. You'll also find salads and sandwiches here. And, yes, there are some impressive dinner choices, such as pasta with scallops, and Gorgonzola cream over filet mignon. But life is short, so eat dessert first — especially at Papa Haydn.

Zell's: An American Café (1300 SE Morrison Street, Buckman, 503-239-0196) hangs its reputation on fresh, fresh scones and strong, strong coffee. For a café, the menu is quite imaginative, with salmon benedict and German pancakes. Filled with old oak tables and chairs from the Arts-and-Crafts era, this "greet the morning" place has a special feeling. Now, be honest: How many eateries can you name that change their breakfast menus seasonally? And at lunchtime — well, that's a whole new menu. Be prepared for long lineups, especially on weekend mornings.

The **Bread and Ink Café** (3610 SE Hawthorne Boulevard, Sunnyside, 503-239-4756, www.breadandinkcafe.com) serves up the best hamburgers in the city. And if that weren't enough to earn it a good reputation, the brunch with blintzes would have the café's name engraved in stone. Ink cartoons right out of the *New Yorker* adorn its pale green walls. Comfortable reading chairs surround paper-covered tables. Relax. No one is going to bother you here for anything more than a coffee refill.

SECRET

CAFFEINE

Portland has more drive-up coffee kiosks than any city I have ever seen. Almost every neighborhood seems to have one, and none seems connected in any way to any other; they're true neighborhood phenomena. Don't look for atmosphere. These are strictly drive-in, fill-up, drive-out establishments — perfect for when you must have a caffeine hit and can't bear to leave the comfort of your car.

Want to get out of your auto? Head for the Mount Tabor neighborhood. This is perk central for Portland, with everything from the ever-present **Starbucks** (3639 SE Hawthorne Boulevard, 503-234-1757) and Portland chain **Coffee People** (3500 SE Hawthorne Boulevard, 503-235-1383), to the cozy **Cup & Saucer Café** (3566 SE Hawthorne Boulevard, 503-236-6001).

If you want to stop and sip a while, try the **Rimsky-Korsakoffee House** (707 SE 12th Avenue, Buckman, 503-232-2640). Conversation and music will greet you at the door of this grand old mansion. The place is almost always packed. Aside from the delectable Café Borgias (coffee, chocolate, and orange flavors all in one cup), you can nibble on desserts and ice cream sundaes. There's not much in the way of signage, so just walk right in and pretend you're one of the regulars.

For a down-home cup of joe (if your home was hippie-era San Francisco), **Common Grounds Coffeehouse** (4321 SE Hawthorne Boulevard, Sunnyside, 503-236-4835) is worth the wait. Yes, you will find lineups out the door. The tables are a little close together and the couches are a little worn, but the magazine rack is full, the coffee is delicious, and there's nothing timid about the dessert case.

Barista (539 NW 13th Avenue, The Pearl, www.baristapdx.com) will take your caffeine consciousness to a whole new level. Billy Wilson, one of the city's favorite baristas has opened his own business, appropriately named for his profession, and — gasp! — featuring coffees from more than one roasting house! The only exclusive arrangement here is to provide very select and very deluxe coffee to the true connoisseur . . . no bargains, just great coffee. You can pay up to $10 for a 10 oz. cup.

SECRET
CAJUN
❧

Ready for some adventure? **Le Bistro Montage** (301 SE Morrison Street, Buckman, 503-234-1324, www.montageportland.com) is a longtime favorite of Portlanders from every walk of life. Eating here is more like a night at the theater (Monty Python comes to mind) than a culinary outing. You'll most likely be seated at a long table with complete strangers, and the service can be sassy. Most of the dishes on the menu involve garlic and noodles. Lots of garlic. Make sure to ask for an oyster shooter. Actually, just yell out "Oystahs!" to the kitchen. Skip the desserts; Le Bistro is not strong in this area. PS: This is possibly the only microbrew-free zone in the city. Only two beers — Rainier and Mickey's — are served at Le Bistro, in the bottle.

SECRET

CAMPING

The only real secret about camping in Portland, or Oregon for that matter, is that it's very wise to reserve in advance for the peak times in summer. For camping spaces on Mount Hood, a reservation is doubly important. For all of Oregon, call 800-452-5687; for Mount Hood, call 503-666-0700.

SECRET

CDs

Crossroads (3130B SE Hawthorne Boulevard, Sunnyside, 503-232-1767, www.xro.com) has stolen a brilliant idea from the antique malls — it's a cooperative of more than 30 music vendors in a storefront. This is the place to begin your search for that elusive Beatles album to complete your collection, as they specialize in hard-to-find music.

Don't know the name of the tune, but you can hum a few bars? The staff at **Music Millennium** (3158 E Burnside Street, Laurelhurst, 503-231-8926, www.musicmillennium.com) can almost always identify the artist. Expect to pay a little more — this *is* a store on "trendy-third" avenue.

Three Sixty Vinyl (214 SW 8th Street, Downtown, 503-224-3688) is the place to find everything in music from experimental to reggae, hip hop to a capella; this is the place to discover music from the edge. It's also a good source of books, magazines, and CDs both new and used.

If you have time to plow through a maze of racks and boxes, **2nd Avenue Records** (400 SW 2nd Avenue, Downtown, 503-222-3783) can give you the time of your life. Rap, metal, alternative, punk, and rock crowd almost every square inch of space in this store.

SECRET
CHAMBER MUSIC

"Quiet, please" is just about the last thing you will hear at **Chamber Music on Tap**. This innovative series of extremely casual chamber music concerts features performances by members of the Oregon Symphony Orchestra and other local musicians of note. Held at the **BridgePort Brewing Company** (1313 NW Marshall Street, The Pearl, 503-241-3612, see "Secret Brews"), the concerts provide audience members with the opportunity to socialize — okay, talk — while the musicians are playing, and to enjoy a good brew and some pizza. This may be the best way ever concocted to get your blue-jeans, blue-collar friends to enjoy a classical concert. And, by the way: Who decided that listening to good music required a formal setting? This series breaks all the rules and creates some much-needed new ones.

CHEAP EATS

Downtown? Hungry? Head to the **Food Carts** at Southwest Alder Street, between 9th and 10th or South West Fifth Avenue between Oak and Stark Streets. Don't let the name deceive you, these are more coffee wagons than simple carts and the menu choices will astonish you. Depending on your location you can choose from almost every cuisine imaginable from Bahamian to Thai. Try the Tabor, with its famous "schnitzelwich" (schnitzel prepared meats stuffed between bread) or choose from any of the many taquerias, thai noodles carts, or just good ol' hotdog stands.

La Buca (40 NE 28th Avenue, 503-238-1058) was the brainchild of Scott Mapes. After abandoning his street-side panini cart in the summer of 1995, he took some time to find just the right location for his next venture. Once he found it, Mapes began to create a new neighborhood eatery in an Italian vein. The menu is the same for both lunch and dinner — pasta dishes such as tomatoey penne puttanesca, and grilled panini sandwiches filled with salami, roasted peppers, and fontina cheese. The atmosphere is simple, uncluttered, and quiet. Most importantly, the food is a good deal.

Open late every night, **Dots Café** (2521 SE Clinton Street, Hosford-Abernethy, 503-235-0203) is a mainstay for locals and bohemian wannabes. Everything here is cooked to order, so be patient. After all, you're not spending the family fortune. The hand-patted burgers are big and juicy, and the fries come in lots of flavors — try the jalapeño, but be sure to order some liquid extinguisher to go with them. At the end of the meal, your server will leave a handful of Jolly Rancher candies with your bill.

It's shabby, but it's good. **Nicholas Restaurant** (318 SE Grand Avenue, Buckman, 503-235-5123) has sacrificed chic for good food. Look past the Spartan, almost sterile, interior and you'll discover that satisfying your palate is more important than the palette of colors on the walls. The falafel is nicely spiced, the pizza is thin and crisp, and the meze platter with hummus, eggplant, grape leaves, and pita will require that at least one friend be with you to finish it.

Another good place for cheap and satisfying food is **McCormick and Schmick's Fish House** (235 SW 1st Avenue, Downtown, 503-224-7522), where $1.95 gets you a great burger. There are other items for the same low price.

S E C R E T
CHEFS

For a different culinary experience, go to the **Chef's Corner** at the Western Culinary Institute (1235 SW Jefferson Street, 503-242-2433), where chefs-in-training cook and serve meals to those with adventurous and understanding taste buds. A five-course lunch goes for about $10, so it's a really good deal. Reservations are required.

SECRET
CHIC
❦

Does Portland have a dress code? Darn right it does. Think fleece, berber, cotton, and Birkenstocks. The rule of thumb is to dress for comfort and walking. You'll see lots of nose rings and tattoos, and spiked hair with gothic dress is pretty common as well. But the overall theme seems to be split between urban hippie and urban sleek. Really, in this city, anything goes.

SECRET
CHILDREN
❦

Since you obviously can't park the children all day with the concierge, or even a reluctant relative, the best thing to do is bring them along. Some of the best places in Portland are quite child friendly. Many of them, like good Disney movies, have two levels of enjoyment: one for children and one for adults.

Portland has some terrific educational activities and museums, such as the **Oregon Museum of Science and Industry**, known locally as "OMSI" (see "Secret Science"), that delight both old and young at heart; a clean downtown full of water fountains for drinking and playing; and kid-friendly amusement parks, zoos, theaters, and stores.

Since I'm no longer under the age of 12, I decided to bring in some outside consultants for this section — my nieces and nephews, who cooperatively gave me the following list of the places to which they would most like to be taken in Portland.

Does one of your children secretly wish to be Michael Andretti? Take him or her to **Malibu Raceway** (9405 SW Cascade Avenue, Beaverton, Oregon, 503-641-8122, www.maliburaceway.com) for a quick spin. Children can drive one of two machines — a slick car or a sprint car. The only requirement is that the child must be at least four feet, six inches tall. The slick cars are the hares and the sprint cars are the turtles on this track. Better to start slow and work up to speed. There's also a two-seater, called a grand barrage, for licensed drivers over 18, which can accommodate young passengers at least three feet, six inches tall. This allows the littlest ones to participate too. The laps can get expensive, so be prepared to spend some serious money. There can also be a long wait for track time.

Crave something with a water element? The **North Clackamas Aquatic Park** (7300 SE Harmony Road, Milwaukie, Oregon, 503-557-SURF) is a water wonderland. There are five pools, as well as giant water slides, a tunnel slide, diving boards, a whirlpool for adults, a wave pool, and sprinkling fountains for the little tykes. This is a terrific place to go on a wintry rainy day, as all of this watery fun is indoors!

One of the oldest children's museums in the country became one of the newest in the summer of 2001 when the **Portland Children's Museum** (4105 SW Canyon Road, Washington Park, 503-223-6500, www.portlandcm.org) opened. This lively, interactive, and engaging museum has managed to find that fine balance between keeping little ones amused and older ones excited. Younger children give high ratings to the flying mops in the *WaterWorks* exhibit; the marimba footbridge, which emits a different tone for every wooden slat you step on; and the Wally Gator chair (which looks like an alligator) in the make-believe dental office. Older kids like *Mirror Mirror*, which allows children to temporarily change their image using reflection, photography, and costumes; and *Me and My Shadow*, a blank-canvas performance space with light projectors and other technology that children can manipulate.

The award-winning **Oregon Zoo** (4001 sw Canyon Road, Washington Park, 503-226-1561, www.oregonzoo.org) has African grassland and rain forest exhibits, a renowned Asian elephant program (see "Secret Elephants"), and one of the largest chimpanzee exhibits in the United States. The *Great Northwest* exhibit features white mountain goats and Steller's sea lions.

Kids of all ages love huge ship locks, especially when they're lucky enough to see a ship passing through. At the **Bonneville Dam** (I-84, exit 40, 541-374-8820), you can also peer through windows at fish ladders to see the powerful salmon struggle to climb upriver to their spawning grounds in spring and summer. Since 9/11, access has been restricted at times, so call ahead first.

Other suggestions from my panel included **Oaks Park** (see "Secret Amusements"), snowboarding on **Mount Hood** (see "Secret Backyard"), **Lloyd Center Ice Rink** (see "Secret Skating"), **Sauvie Island** for a day at the beach (see "Secret Island"), and **Things From Another World** (see "Secret Aliens").

SECRET

CHOCOLATE

For a city the size of Portland, there is a remarkable amount of chocolate manufacturing going on here. **Verdun Fine Chocolate** (421

NW 10th Avenue, The Pearl, 503-525-9400, www.verdunchocolates
.com) has created a "Tiffany-like" atmosphere for a chocolate shop.
Delicious Lebanese chocolates (that's right, chocolate from Lebanon)
are wrapped and presented exquisitely. For special events you can
even have individual wrappings created — perfect for weddings,
reunions, birthdays, or anniversaries.

Van Duyn's Chocolates (2360 NW Quimby Street, Northwest,
503-227-1927; 12000 SE 82nd Avenue, 503-659-1031; and 1212 Lloyd
Center, 503-281-2421; www.vanduyns.com) has been creating delightful confectionary concoctions for decades. Step inside the small,
ivy-covered shop, fronted by a deep blue door, and sample the most
decadent bit of Rocky Road that you have ever tried. Just one bite
and you will know why making your own marshmallow makes a
difference.

The Candy Basket (1924 NE 181st Avenue, Gresham, Oregon, 503-
666-2000, www.candybasketinc.com) greets you with a cascading
"chocolate fall" of 2,800 pounds of melted chocolate oozing over
21 feet of marble and bronze sculpture. It's a truly mouthwatering
sight and, as far as we and the Candy Basket know, the only one of
its kind in the world. You are asked not to sample from the cascade
but to come inside for a try. The Candy Basket creates all kinds of
specialty chocolates and ships them worldwide. You can buy bags of
"seconds" at a discount.

JaCiva's Chocolates (4733 SE Hawthorne Boulevard, Sunnyside,
503-234-8115, www.jacivas.com) has been serving up handmade
chocolates and divine desserts in this location for more than 20 years.
There's a tiny sitting area where you can munch a goodie, but most
of the chocolates and cakes are sold for taking home.

Moonstruck Chocolatier (6600 N Baltimore Avenue, 800-557-

MOON, www.moonstruckchocolate.com) conjures up chocolate wizardry by the pound. Don't blame those extra hip inches on me — you could have skipped this section.

SECRET

CHRISTMAS

The **Macy's Holiday Parade** (503-241-3900) on Thanksgiving Day officially launches the holiday season. The parade lineup is a West Coast feast that includes the sw Washington Llama Association, Miss Molalla Buckeroo and the Rodeo Bandits, and the Pacific Festival Ballet. The parade typically begins at NW 8th and Davis, and follows Broadway from Davis to sw Alder, where marchers turn and head for sw 3rd. After a short distance on 3rd, the parade proceeds up sw Taylor and finally disbands at Lincoln High School.

Meanwhile, over at the **Portland International Raceway** (1940 N Victory Boulevard, Bridgeton, 503-823-RACE, www.portlandraceway .com), lights and animation spark the night in what is billed as the largest drive-through light show in the Northwest. The **Pittock Mansion** (3229 NW Pittock Drive, Washington Park, 503-823-3623 or 503-823-3624, pittockmansion.org, see "Secret Mansion") joins in the festivities with an extravagantly decorated Victorian home and grounds. And the **Festival of Lights at the Grotto** (NE 85th Avenue and Sandy Boulevard, Roseway, 503-254-7371, see "Secret Grotto") features a light show and living history pageant.

The **RiverPlace Hotel** (1510 sw Harbor Way, Downtown, 503-228-3233 or 800-227-1333, www.riverplacehotel.com) is Portland's only hotel on the Willamette River, and thus it has a perfect view of the city's annual **Christmas Boat Parade**.

Can't wait until the holiday season to begin your holiday decorating? Head for the lower level of the **Troutdale General Store** (289 E Historic Columbia River Highway, 503-492-7912, Troutdale). Descend the stairs to discover holiday heaven. Christmas takes center stage but you can find Easter, Halloween, Valentine's Day and even the 4th of July well represented with decorations, tchotchkes, and all sorts of décor you really don't need but want.

Are you in the city during the holiday season and just can't bear the thought of braving the traffic-laden malls? Head for the airport. Powell's Books, Made In Oregon, tie and scarf stores, a Nike outlet, and several other shops make it an excellent and secret location for Christmas shopping. You don't have to clear security for this part of the airport, and if you don't mind leaping over bags with wheels, it's a lot less hectic than some of the other malls at Christmastime. Now that the MAX train goes straight to the terminal, you don't even have to find a parking space.

Every evening (except Christmas Eve and Christmas Day) from late November until just after Christmas, the **Oregon Zoo** (4001 SW Canyon Road, Washington Park, 503-226-1561) lights up like a Christmas tree for their annual extravaganza, **Zoolights**. This spectacular event transforms the zoo into a wonderland, decorated with nearly one million lights. Illuminated monkeys swing through trees, frogs leap when you least expect it. This is truly a community event as the festival brings together local musicians and dancers. Be sure to take the zoo train, which is also brightly decorated for the event.

Christmas at the Zoo (118 NW 23rd Avenue, Northwest, 503-223-

4048, www.christmasatthezoo.com) is not what you think. This intriguing shop is filled with holiday decorations and stuffed animals. You may not find something to put on the tree (just try not to!) but you will certainly discover something to put under it, or in a stocking.

Oregon is proudly the source for grand Christmas trees nationwide, often including the White House Christmas tree and the National Christmas Tree in Washington, D.C. In Portland's Pioneer Square, the illumination of a 75-foot tree heralds the beginning of the festive season in the city complete with Santa Claus and music.

SECRET
CHRONICLES

The **Visual Chronicle of Portland** is the only public art collection of its kind in the United States. It's a city-owned archival collection of works on paper. These works portray the artists' ideas, visions, and perceptions of what makes Portland such a unique city, and are on display throughout City Hall (1221 SW 4th Avenue, Downtown).

SECRET
CITIZENS

Who calls Portland home? Author and cooking teacher James Beard; Beverly Cleary, author of the Ramona books; author Jean Auel; cartoonist Matt Groening of *Simpsons* fame; Phil Knight, founder of Nike; John Reed, socialist and activist; filmmaker Gus Van Sant (part time these days); Will Vinton, creator of the California Raisins; and Dr. Linus Pauling, Nobel Prize–winning scientist and vitamin C advocate.

SECRET
CLUB SCENE
❖

Portland's night scene has grown explosively with the gentrification of Old Town Chinatown and The Pearl, as well as growth in eastern neighborhoods. The city has been undergoing a musical renaissance on many levels — punk, jazz, alternative, and blues. Couple that with perhaps the best beer on the West Coast, and you've got yourself a night scene of which you can be proud.

Want to dress to impress and have the right venue to show off your finery? You want to be seen on the scene at **Paragon** (1309 NW Hoyt Street, The Pearl, 503-833-5060), possibly the hippest hangout in town. This club pays homage to its industrial roots with a sort of Edward-Hopper-in-the-new-century ambiance. There is live music on Wednesday and Thursday nights and a DJ on Fridays and Saturdays.

Saucebox (214 SW Broadway, Downtown, 503-241-3393, www.saucebox.com) is another of the city's currently popular places to be seen. This downtown restaurant/club is a large, dramatically lit dark box that can be extremely noisy. So if you plan to have any significant conversations, make sure you do so before 10 PM, when the DJ arrives to turn the restaurant into a dance club.

Do you think innocent, sometimes stuck-in-the-'60s Portland is without a punk scene? Think again. **Club Satyricon** (125 NW 6th Avenue, Old Town Chinatown, www.myspace.com/satyricon.pdx) is one of the oldest underground music venues and offers plenty of punk. It's just about the only place in town to catch the subterranean buzz bands of yesterday and today.

Tired of the same old clubs? Want to gyrate to something more enthralling than current radio pap? **The Ohm** (31 NW 1st Avenue, Old Town Chinatown, 503-241-2916) is a slick, Miami-style club with a surprisingly excellent sound system. The club's weekly Aqualounge offers hours of non-stop break beats and dance tracks in which to lose yourself. The Ohm is a late-night treat — good music, good food, and lots of energy. But beware: the cover charge is a little high and the service is not always as nice as it could be.

Berbati's Pan (231 SW Ankeny Street, Downtown, 503-226-2122, www.berbati.com) grew out of the popular Berbati's Restaurant almost as an afterthought. Once tiny, it has now grown in size and prominence over the last few years. What makes it so hip? A large dance floor, live music, separate pool and game rooms — and, most importantly, ping-pong during happy hours. (Oops, there are no happy hours in Portland. The state liquor board ruled them a no-no. But you will find the odd place for attitude adjustment.)

SECRET
COCKTAILS

Want to play dress-up? The **Benson Hotel Lobby Court** (309 SW Broadway, Downtown, 503-228-2000, www.bensonhotel.com)

is a fun place to go and have a drink. Wear your slinkiest best and pretend you're waiting for Bill and Hillary to join you at any moment. The lobby is dark and lined with imported Russian walnut, sometimes called Circassian, and lush comfortable chairs. The bar offers 28 kinds of martinis — one for every day of the month, in February. There's also some gentle jazz that plays Tuesday through Saturday.

Driftwood (Hotel deLuxe, 729 sw 15th Avenue, Downtown, 503-223-6311, www.hoteldeluxe.com) is a cocktail mixed straight from the Golden era of Hollywood. This snug little lounge tucked into a corner of the Hotel deLuxe is a perfect place for moguls to chat up starlets. The drinks are generous and the appetizers may make you want to miss dinner. Nibble on oysters on the half shell, grilled shrimp, or seared ahi.

Sink into a deep red booth at **The Gilt Club** (306 NW Broadway, Downtown, 503-222-4458, www.giltclub.com) and let the luscious charm of this over-the-top, overdone, but oh-so-right, cocktail emporium surround you. For those nights when you really want to be a grownup or maybe a James Bond wannabe, this is your haunt.

Good eats and cocktails in an automotive atmosphere is the slogan of **Duff's Garage** (1635 SE 7th Avenue, Downtown, 503-234-BEER, www.duffsgarage.com). There's also plenty of live music in this funky bar, which caters to a wider audience than grease monkeys, although mechanical types will be quite at home here.

SECRET

COLLEGES

You probably know about the big schools in the city — Portland State University and Reed College (haven for future intelligentsia) — but there's lots of learning going on elsewhere in this city, too.

For example, there's the **Oregon College of Oriental Medicine** (10525 Cherry Blossom Drive, Montavilla, 503-253-3443, www.ocom .edu). The college presents programs in all aspects of traditional Oriental medicine, including the theory and practice of acupuncture, herbal medicine, traditional Chinese physic-therapy and qi cultivation, and basics such as anatomy, pharmacology, and public and community health.

The **Portland College of Legal Arts** (8909 sw Barbur Boulevard, 503-928-3431, www.collegeoflegalarts.edu) was formerly known as the Court Reporting Institute. In 1986, the college expanded its scope, and now it offers a legal secretarial and paralegal/legal assistance program. You can also learn how to be a correctional officer. Don't forget: crime does appear to be a growth industry these days.

The **Oregon College of Art and Craft** (8245 sw Barnes Road, West Haven Neighborhood, Beaverton, Oregon, 503-297-5544, www.ocac.edu) traces its origins to 1907, when Julia Hoffman founded the Arts and Crafts Society. The society educated the public on the value of arts and crafts in daily life through art classes and exhibitions that featured the best examples of American crafts. Today, the college is an accredited craft college teaching classes in book arts, ceramics, drawing, fibers, metal, photography, and metal-

and wood-working. There's no place for your glue gun here — this is the complex stuff.

S E C R E T
COLUMBIA

As you go through this volume, you'll probably notice that I've paid a lot more attention to the Willamette River than to the Columbia. You see, contrary to common belief, Portland does not lie on the Columbia River. It lies on the Willamette River, at the point where it intersects the Columbia. Having established that, I'd like to tell you a little bit about why the Columbia River has been so very, very important to this region.

The Columbia River, 1,214 miles long, is the fourth-largest river in the United States and the 18th-largest river in the world. It carries 10 times as much water as the Colorado and more than twice as much as the Nile. At one time, with annual salmon runs of 6 to 10 million, the Columbia was home to more salmon than any other place on earth. Unfortunately, because of dams, cattle grazing, and logging, those numbers are seriously declining.

The Columbia rises in the Selkirk Mountains of British Columbia and wanders through eastern and central Washington, where it flows over and through numerous dams. It cuts deep through the Columbia River Gorge and passes one last hurdle, the Bonneville Dam, before continuing the last 146 miles to the ocean.

SECRET

COMFORT FOOD

With a name like **Mother's Bistro and Bar** (212 SW Stark Street, 503-464-1122, www.mothersbistro.com), what else would you expect but good, old-fashioned, down-home cooking like Mom used to make? That's what you'll find here — if your mother was a professional chef. All kidding aside, Mother's features world-Mom signature dishes, such as pot roast, meatloaf, chicken and dumplings, and cioppino. Everything is made from scratch — salads, soups, homemade biscuits, and desserts.

Owner-chef Lisa Schroeder says: "Over the years, I have come to realize that home-cooked food is the best food. I'm talking about the kind of foods our mothers and grandmothers used to make when they had time. Slow-cooked foods that take hours to prepare — stews, roasts, and braised dishes. At Mother's, we take classic homemade favorites and refine them with classical cooking techniques, so they're like mom's cooking, only maybe a little better."

Portland agrees that this is better than mom's cooking — *Willamette Week* newspaper chose Mother's Bistro as Restaurant of the Year in 2002.

SECRET

COPPER

Portlandia is the second-largest hammered-copper statue in the world (the Statue of Liberty is the largest). In 1985, the citizenry came to cheer as the sculpture was barged down the Willamette River, hauled through downtown, and then lifted three stories to a ledge on the Portland Building (5th Avenue and Madison Street, Downtown). Why *Portlandia*? Why a sculpture of a woman? The art is based on Lady Commerce, a figure on the city's seal. Critics have called the work of sculptor Raymond Kaskey everything from brilliant to hideous. Go have a look at the kneeling giantess and draw your own conclusion.

SECRET

COWBOYS AND COWGIRLS

Admit it. Every since you saw *City Slickers* with Billy Crystal, you've wanted to run off, be a cowboy or cowgirl, and rescue a lost calf. Well, you'll need to go outside Portland for this undertaking. The **Long Hollow Ranch** (71105 Holmes Road, Sisters, Oregon, 877-923-1901, www.lhranch.com) operates from June to September. Its Bed & Breakfast is open from September to December and from March to June. You can ride Oregon's high desert and soak in a hot tub. This round-up is strictly for adults; children are not allowed.

The **Aspen Ridge Resort** (Bly, Oregon, 800-393-3323, www.aspenrr .com) is a working ranch with 1,000 head of cattle on 14,000 acres. It also has swimming and tennis facilities, just in case you tire of the cowhand routine. Aspen Ridge is open from April to February, in case you like your ranch experience with a touch of snow.

SECRET

CROSSINGS

Portland, to state the obvious, is a city of bridges: 17, to be precise, including the world's only telescoping double-deck vertical-lift bridge (Steel Bridge), the world's oldest vertical-lift bridge (Hawthorne Bridge), and America's longest tied-arch bridge (Fremont Bridge). Goodness, who knew there were so many kinds! If you were to arrive in the city by boat, heading inland along the Willamette, you would encounter some of the city's most famous spans in the following order.

The **St. Johns Bridge** is named for the community at its east end, which was originally named in honor of settler James John. John started a local ferry system near this spot with just one rowboat in 1852. Portland's only suspension bridge was designed by David B. Steinman, and the architect considered this Gothic-towered creation to be his masterpiece.

The **Fremont Bridge**, the newest to span the Willamette River, has the longest main span of any bridge in Oregon. The bridge was named in honor of John Charles Fremont, explorer and army officer. In 1842, Fremont was given federal funds to survey the Oregon Trail.

The **Broadway Bridge**, when it opened, was the longest double-leaf drawbridge in the world. Its appellation reflects the street it carries. The city fathers spared no imagination in the naming of this viaduct.

The unique design of the **Steel Bridge** has never been duplicated. It features two decks, one for trains and one for automobiles, the lower of which can move independently of the other. Not only does this bridge accommodate wheeled vehicles, it also obliges river traffic.

The lower deck can be raised 45 feet in only 10 seconds; the upper deck, 90 feet in 90 seconds. Talk about zero to 60! Before the mid-century decline in streetcar use, the upper deck was used for Portland's streetcars. In 1986, following an upgrade, the Steel Bridge became the cross-river link for Portland's MAX light-rail system.

The **Burnside Bridge** closes for a few hours each June to allow the Grand Floral Parade of the Portland Rose Festival to cross the river en route to downtown. The **Morrison Bridge**, part of the Willamette Light Brigade's project to light all the downtown bridges, was the first to be illuminated in 1987.

The **Marquam Bridge** holds the honor of being Portland's busiest span. It was the first double-deck automobile bridge to be built in the state. Built for utility rather than beauty, this connection closed the final gap in the California–Washington interstate highway system.

Only the interstate bridges cross the Columbia River.

S E C R E T
CYCLING
✤

In March 1999, *Bicycling* magazine ranked Portland second on its list of the "Ten Best Cycling Cities in North America." New bike lanes are continually being added to city streets, and the police department now has a cadre of bike patrollers.

The **Yellow Bikes** are the city's on-again, off-again experiment with free transport — or, as it is better known, bike sharing. The solid yellow cycles can be found (if you are lucky and sharp-eyed) against buildings or trees. Go ahead — take one for a spin around the city. Just be sure to leave it in a conspicuous spot.

Want to pedal your own bike? Pick up a bike-centric map of the city from the **Bicycle Transportation Alliance** (233 NW 5th Avenue, 503-226-0676, www.bta4bikes.org). The Alliance is a great source for the most up-to-date cycling info in the city.

The perfect place for taking an afternoon or morning ride is along "the Waterfront." The **Eastbank Esplanade** has a 1.5-mile pedestrian and cycling trail that extends from the Steel Bridge to the Hawthorne Bridge. This is a very popular place so be prepared to dodge pedestrians and puppies.

Portland's **Pedalpalooza** (www.shift2bikes.org) is the premier family cycling event in the city. Held in early June, this bike extravaganza is perfect for a dad riding a deluxe mountain bike alongside his youngster in a tricked-out tricycle.

Did you ever secretly desire to bare it all when you bicycle? Well get ready to pedal Portland in the altogether. The **World Naked Bike Ride** in Portland attracted almost 5,000 scantily, if at all, clad riders in its last event. Safety vests and helmets are recommended but even those are optional.

Does your bike require some repair? Push it to the **Bicycle Repair Collective** (4438 SE Belmont Street, Sunnyside, 503-233-0564, www.bicyclerepaircol.net). The store sells parts and accessories, and rents work space for repairs. Employees also give classes on bike repair and maintenance. For $50 a year, or $5 an hour, you can tune up your bike.

The **Fat Tire Farm** (2714 NW Thurman Street, Northwest, 503-222-FARM, www.fattirefarm.com) is where mountain-biker wannabes flock to rent bikes and helmets. Oh, yeah, you can buy stuff here, too: bike accessories, clothes, literature, and miscellany.

If it's too tiring to cycle all over the city, you can purchase a $5 permit to carry your bike on TriMet buses and MAX trains. Pick up a permit at the **TriMet office** (Pioneer Courthouse Square, Downtown, 503-238-RIDE).

SECRET

DANCING

Country and western, contra, English country, Irish ceili, square, or ballroom — you can find it on a floor in Portland. Need a little afternoon jive? The **Swing Street Band** plays every Thursday at the **Pioneer Community Center** (615 5th Street, Oregon City, 503-657-8287).

Like your dancing in a line? Then head to — I'm not kidding! — the **Ponderosa Lounge at the Jubitz Truck Stop** (10350 N Vancouver Way, Bridgeton, 503-345-0300, www.ponderosalounge.com). Live country-and-western bands play seven nights a week and the place really jumps. There are enough cowboys and cowgirls to cast a new version of *Urban Cowboy*.

SECRET

DIVES

The **Roxy** (1121 sw Stark Street, Downtown, 503-223-9160) is like a juke joint that shaved its head and joined a punk band. But it is open 24 hours a day, so if you need some post-party nutrients, you'll find all the grease and salt you want. Don't be put off by the sea of black T-shirts and jangling chains — there are nice, tall, comfy booths to sink into while you thumb through the big, bookish menu. Want to really pig out? Order the "poo poo platter" — nuggets of clams, shrimp, chicken, onion rings, and fries. It's a heart attack on a plate.

There's no delicate way to put this: **Lydia's Restaurant** (18330 E Burnside Street, Gresham, Oregon, 503-666-2516) is a dive. But it's a great dive. A dark and smoky interior. A dance floor the size of a postage stamp. Why should you go there? The food is terrific. The two-for-one steak specials are a tasty deal.

SECRET

DOG FRIENDLY

Many hotels, including the upscale **Hotel Monaco** (506 sw Washington Street, Downtown, 503-222-0001 or 888-207-2201, www.monaco-portland.com) and the **Hotel Vintage Plaza** (422 sw Broadway, Downtown, 503-228-1212 or 800-263-2305, www.vintageplaza.com), allow pets. However, only two city parks allow dogs to run off the leash. They are **Gabriel Park** (the off-leash area is at sw 45th Avenue near sw Vermont Street, Hayhurst), and **Chimney Park** (9360 Columbia Boulevard, St. Johns).

SECRET
DOUGHNUTS

Portland has its very own doughnut — the Portland Crème, named for one of the founders who was from Portland, Maine. Created by the owners of **Voodoo Doughnuts** (22 sw 3rd Avenue, Downtown, 503-241-4704, voodoodoughnut.com), the Portland Crème sports two beady little eyes and an impish tongue. You'll have to look long and far to find a doughnut this good. The owners create special doughnuts for special occasions and you can even hold your wedding ceremony — or simply a ceremony of intention — in the shop.

SECRET
DRIVING RULES

Don't you wonder every time you visit a new place whether you can turn right on a red light? In Portland, you can, after you come to a full stop. Also, if you are in the far left lane of a one-way street, you may turn left onto another one-way street at a red light after, again, coming to a full stop.

You already do this, I know, but in Oregon everyone in a moving vehicle is required to wear a seat belt.

SECRET

ELEPHANTS

More Asian elephants (28 to date) have been born in Portland's **Oregon Zoo** (4001 sw Canyon Road, Washington Park, 503-226-1561, www .oregonzoo.org) than in any other North American facility. It began with Packy, the first Asian elephant born in the western hemisphere. That blessed event blazed the way for a pachyderm maternity program. Now, with more than two dozen newborns to the zoo's credit (including one third-generation pachyderm), the elephant program continues.

Make sure you don't miss the Elephant Museum, which takes a lighthearted look at pachyderm portrayals throughout history. Along with elephant jokes, you'll find elephants in literature and art depicted with dioramas and masks. A look at the ivory trade injects a somber note into the proceedings.

However, there's a lot more to see than pregnant elephants! The zoo has a complex chimpanzee exhibit, and an African savannah that features black rhinoceros, giraffes, impalas, and zebras. The African rainforest exhibit produces hourly rainstorms and displays more than two dozen animal species. My favorite is the exhibit of Peruvian Humboldt penguins. The colony was endangered, but here it thrives in a protected environment.

At the newest exhibit, *The Great Northwest*, visitors can journey through mountain forests and lush coastlines to view Steller sea lions, wolverines, black bears, and bald eagles.

Psst...on the second Tuesday of each month, admission is free after 1 PM.

S E C R E T

ENVY

You wouldn't suspect that laid-back Portland would have a jealous bone in its collective body, but there are some things that Portlanders secretly envy about Seattle. They envy the pro sport franchises of the Mariners and Seahawks, probably because the Trail Blazers seem to end each year out of the playoffs. And they envy Seattle's seemingly booming economy. Portland has its share of big players, such as Nike and Intel, but it can't seem to shake that younger-sibling attitude.

On the other hand, Seattle envies Portland because of three little words: no sales tax.

S E C R E T

EXTREME SPORTS

When the snow melts on Mount Hood, the fun is only beginning. Skibowl has taken advantage of its location, only 50 miles east of Portland, by opening **Action Park** (Route 26, Government Camp, 503-222-2695). This extreme-sport park is a huge success with those who want to mountain bike, race Indy karts, tramp on a trampoline, play miniature and Frisbee golf, "body Nerf," or take advantage of the Velcro Fly Trap or batting cages. Not quite extreme enough? How about the 100-foot freefall bungee tower? Or the 80-foot fling on the reverse rapid-riser bungee jump? You see, you can go to Mount Hood, not ski, and *still* manage to break something.

A little closer to town, you can try rock climbing at the **Portland Rock Gym** (21 NE 12th Avenue, Hosford-Abernethy, 503-232-8310, www.portlandrockgym.com). This is just the ticket for the adventurer who can't keep his or her feet on the ground. The walls vary in height and can be set to challenge advanced or novice climbers. Really a novice? There are lessons available.

SECRET

FESTIVALS

Portland is a city that likes to have a good time. You couldn't exactly call it party central, but it certainly serves up its share of feasts, fêtes, and festivals all year long. Family, ethnic, culinary, traditional, whimsical, jazzy — you name it and you'll find an occasion to fit the bill.

In February, just when we all need a little sunshine in our lives, the **Portland International Film Festival** (Northwest Film Center, 934 SW Salmon Street, 503-221-1156, www.nwfilm.org) comes to town with more than 100 films from 30 countries. This rich snapshot of world cinema gives film buffs the opportunity to discover and celebrate movies rarely seen at the multiplex.

The largest **Cinco de Mayo Festival** (503-232-7550, www. cincode mayo.org) held outside Mexico is Portland's celebration of Hispanic culture. The festival also honors Portland's sister city relationship with Guadalajara, Mexico. Governor Tom McCall Waterfront Park is the venue for this Mexican fiesta that features music, entertainment, markets, and, of course, food, food, food!

Parades are just the tip of the rosebud when it comes to the award-winning **Portland Rose Festival** (503-227-2681, www.rosefestival .org). The festival comprises more than 70 events held over several days. The festivities begin with the Rose Festival Queen's coronation, followed by evenings of fireworks, a starlight run for athletes, an evening starlight parade, milk carton boat races, the nation's largest junior parade, the arrival of ships for Fleet Week, a boat festival, dragonboat races, band concerts, an arts festival, an Indy car race, a grand floral parade, and, of course, a rose show.

The Rose Festival *is* Portland. The crowds are amazing, the roses are gorgeous, and even if it rains, everyone still seems to have a wonderful time. The Rose Festival also reminds both residents and visitors that Portland has kept its small-town flair.

Of course, the Rose Festival also coincides with Fleet Week, when the Navy comes to town. Sometimes, even ships from other countries pay a visit. So, if your intention is to go to the city to pick up women, or men, you might want to select another week when the competition won't be quite so stiff.

July brings the **Safeway Waterfront Blues Festival** (503-282-0555, www.waterfrontbluesfest.com) and the **Oregon Brewers Festival** (www.oregonbrewfest.com) to the banks of the river. The Blues Festival is one of the largest in the United States, but what makes this event truly special is that it benefits the Oregon Food Bank. The event features local, national, and international blues artists, along with food and a spectacular fireworks display. At the Brewers Festival, more than 80,000 beer enthusiasts gather to sample about 70 different beers from around the world (that's actually more flavors than you can find in Portland's ample collection of microbreweries).

And what would the holiday season be without lights? In December, three notable Portland sites are ablaze with lights and music. The **Festival of Lights at the Grotto** (NE 85th Avenue and Sandy Boulevard, Roseway, 503-254-7371, pittockmansion.org, see "Secret Grotto") is an amazing display of nearly 150,000 lights that offers a glowing background to the largest choral festival in the Pacific Northwest. The **Zoolights Festival** (4001 SW Canyon Road, Washington Park, 503-226-1561, www.oregonzoo.org) turns the Oregon Zoo into a holiday fairyland, with a decorated train and gingerbread house display. And as for the lights at the **Pittock Mansion** (3229 NW Pittock Drive, Washington Park, 503-823-3623 or 503-823-3624, pittockmansion.org, see "Secret Mansion") — well, who wouldn't love to come home to this Victorian marvel aglow with seasonal warmth?

S E C R E T

FLUFFERNUTTER

This is one of those things adults will not usually confess — a craving for a Fluffernutter sandwich. You know what I mean: peanut butter combined with Marshmallow Fluff. Decadent and calorie laden, this is comfort food straight out of the '50s. If you want or need to find one in the Rose City, head to **Crowsenberg's Half & Half** (923 SW Oak Street, Downtown, 503-222-4495). This luncheonette is almost terminally cute, but it does serve up a divine Fluffernutter sandwich. They even toast it! Yummy!

SECRET

FM

KBOO (FM 90.7, 503-231-8032, www.kboo.org) is an idiosyncratic, non-corporate, counterculture breath of fresh oxygen on the airwaves over the city. During its 14-hour broadcast day, expect the unexpected. KBOO's roots are classical. The non-profit station was formed in 1972 and it has continued to grow in subscribers and broadcast power over the years. Expect to hear music, discussion of controversial issues, arguments for social change, and even a plea for the return of lost pets.

SECRET

FONDUE

Gustav's Bier Stube (5035 NE Sandy Boulevard, Hollywood, 503-288-5503) is waiting to fill you with fondue, sausage, and oom-pah-pah. The ever-full breadbasket of rye and sourdough is a perfect complement to the cheese delights.

SECRET

FORESTS

When Lewis and Clark arrived in Portland nearly 200 years ago, they found a landscape filled with 1,000-year-old grand Douglas firs,

300 feet tall and 10 feet in diameter. Sadly, almost 95 percent of these trees have disappeared. Do not despair. Recent conservation movements made giant leaps in the preservation of old-growth forests. In fact, nearly half of Oregon, or 30 million acres, is forestland. Of that 30 million, 2.2 million acres are federally protected wilderness areas. These areas are designated to remain undisturbed — no roads or motorized vehicles are allowed. In the city, you can find lots of places to walk in the woods and imagine, just for a little while, that you are part of Lewis and Clark's famous expedition.

Hoyt Arboretum (4000 sw Fairview Boulevard, Washington Park, 503-865-8733, www.hoytarboretum.org) is a much-loved space. Covering about 185 ridgetop acres about two miles west of downtown, the arboretum is home to a collection of trees representing more than 1,100 species gathered from around the world. That's a lot of toothpicks waiting to be milled! Twelve miles of trail wind through this living exhibit that includes not only trees but also shrubs. Pick your favorite season to visit and wander through glades of magnolias, cherries, dogwoods, and other blooming species.

For a more global perspective on forests, your best bet is the **World Forestry Center Museum** (4033 sw Canyon Road, Washington Park, 503-228-1367, www.worldforestry.org). The center allows you to explore the Pacific Northwest's unique forested environment; experience the world's rainforests through the Smithsonian exhibit, *Tropical Rainforests: A Disappearing Treasure*; and encounter trees that were alive 200 million years ago in the *Forests of Stone*. All that after you've been greeted by a 70-foot-tall talking tree!

Forest Park (end of nw Thurman Street, at Upshur Street, Northwest, 503-823-7529) is the place to go when you want to hike through the woods all day and never be out of range of a latte. Forest

Park is the granddaddy of all of Portland's parks. It's a true wilderness reserve. With over 5,000 acres and 60 miles of trails through old-growth forest, it's the largest city park in the United States. The park is home to a lot of wildlife, such as elk and black bear, so you may not want to wander too deep into the forest. A good first hike begins at the end of NW Thurman Street. Park your car, walk a short distance on an access road to Wild Cherry Trail, then continue on Wildwood Trail. From there, head onto Aspen Trail, which eventually will lead you back to Thurman Street and your car. Is that too much for you? Then park in the lot at NW Upshur Street and walk along the easy trail amid the ancient trees. When you've had your fill of Mother Nature, head back to your car and the nearest Starbucks.

SECRET

FOUNTAINS

Portland owes its "refreshing" atmosphere to lumber baron and philanthropist Simon Benson. While walking through his mill one day, Benson noticed the smell of alcohol on his workers' breath. When Benson asked the men why they drank in the middle of the day, they replied there was no fresh drinking water to be found downtown. Upon hearing this, Benson proceeded to commission 20 elegant freshwater drinking fountains, now known as the **Benson Bubblers**. Beer consumption in the city reportedly decreased 25 percent after the fountains were installed. Today, you can still drink from the Benson Bubblers in the downtown area. Like the Art Nouveau metro signs in Paris, the bubblers add an elegant touch to the sidewalk scenario.

The tradition of fountains for the city lives on in Governor Tom Mc-Call Waterfront Park with the **Salmon Street Springs**. This fountain was designed to celebrate city life. Its 185 jets are programmed to change with the city's moods (it's a good thing it's not programmed to change with my moods, or it would be the most rapid-fire fountain in the universe!). At full capacity, the fountain recycles 4,924 gallons of water per minute. Kids — and adults — love to splash around and cool off here on hot summer days.

When the **Skidmore Fountain** (sw 1st Avenue, at Ankeny Street, Downtown) opened in 1888, brewer Henry Weinhard offered to pump beer from his brewery (via Portland's fire hoses) into the fountain's pipes. This festive suggestion was vetoed, however, by the city's leaders, who feared residents would help themselves to the beer by poking holes in the fire hoses. So today, as on opening day, the Skidmore Fountain runs with water. The fountain's upper bowl is supported by four female figures. The bottom pool, once a place for residents to quench their thirst, still has the brass rings that held community copper cups. Four lower troughs, filled by spillover from the bottom pool, were designed for the convenience of dogs and horses. This fountain, which is the oldest piece of public art in the city, is inscribed, "Good Citizens are the Riches of a City."

And then there is the **Untitled Fountain** (sw 6th Avenue at Pine Street, Downtown), locally dubbed "the car wash." This tubular fountain has been known to send sprays in all directions, so on particularly gusty days a wind gauge turns the fountain off.

SECRET

FREE RIDES

In downtown Portland, the free public transit ride (or **fareless square**) stretches from the west bank of the river in Old Town Chinatown past Pioneer Courthouse Square to SW 13th Avenue on the west side of downtown, extending all the way to the Lloyd Center on the east. You'll need a ticket for the rest of the system. Fares depend on how far you travel and are issued on an honor basis. If a conductor asks to see your ticket, you had better be able to produce one or you'll face a hefty fine. Each station has machines that can make change and validate tickets. The tickets are good for a specified period of time, in any direction. For more information, contact TriMet, Portland's transit company (503-238-RIDE, www.trimet.org).

SECRET

FREEBIES

The best things in life are free, and a visit to Portland is no exception. Some of the city's foremost attractions will cost you nothing, zip, nada. Let me name a few: **Pioneer Courthouse Square**, the city's "living room" in the center of town (see "Secret Squares"); **Portland Saturday Market**, which is open on Sundays, too (see "Secret Saturdays"); Washington Park, the site of the **International Rose Test Garden** (see "Secret Gardens"); **First Thursday**, a city-wide art extravaganza (see "Secret Thursdays"); **Mount Tabor Park**, a dormant volcanic cone within the city limits (see "Secret Volcanoes"); and **Sauvie Island**, for swimming, picnicking, and berry picking (see "Secret Island").

SECRET

FRENCH

Are you ready for a little ooh-la-la in your life? Head for a French restaurant that won't break your budget. **Le Bouchon** (517 NW 14th Avenue, Old Town Chinatown, 503-248-2193) serves up traditional French fare. The tables are a little close together and the service could use some improvement. But, if you close your eyes, you could feel as though you were in Paris.

Fenouil (900 NW 11th Avenue, The Pearl, 503-525-2225, www .fenouilinthepearl.com) is the most elegant French restaurant Portland has seen in quite some time. Located in the ever-trendy Pearl District, this upscale brasserie focuses on Mediterranean cuisine. You'll find frogs' legs served with bagna cuda, seared scallops, steak frites, and other French delights both familiar and new.

You'll find a "French-inspired" menu at **Le Pigeon** (738 E Burnside Street, Buckman, 503-546-8796, www.lepigeon.com). The menu may surprise you with the pork belly, artichoke and anchovy appetizer, or the entrée of fennel crèpes. But what really sets this restaurant apart from its French contenders is that the dining is communal or a seat at the bar. Head somewhere else for romance; Le Pigeon is for those who enjoy good food and lots of company.

The **Brasserie Montmartre** (626 SW Park Avenue, Downtown, 503-224-5552) is both fun loving and romantic. It's a little taste of Paris,

with its black-and-white checkered floors, old-fashioned lamps, and even a little raised stage where live jazz is performed nightly. The colorful drawings on the wall are worth your attention, too: they are the results of the Brasserie's annual coloring contest. (All of the tables are covered in butcher paper and you're offered handfuls of crayons on your arrival so that you, too, can create a masterpiece while you await your meal.) The fare is simple, but interesting: french-fried artichoke hearts with sweet dill mustard, broiled filet mignon with peppercorn sauce, and saffron angel hair pasta with garlic, garlic, garlic. The desserts are almost too decadent to contemplate, so make sure you leave room for one.

SECRET

GALLERIES

Art galleries are known to change hands frequently, so the best place to begin an art quest in Portland is in The Pearl or the downtown core. The Pearl, which was once an aging and abandoned industrial center, has been revitalized in recent years and has become a center for art in the city. The neighborhood, located roughly between Burnside Street and NW 10th and 14th avenues, is filled with galleries, artists' lofts, restaurants, and art-oriented businesses. You'll also find a handful of antique stores. There are oodles of galleries along the streets of Downtown's Yamhill District and Old Town-Chinatown's Skidmore District. You could spend days in Portland's galleries; there were more than 100 at last count.

Both of these areas are particularly alive on **First Thursday** (see

"Secret Thursdays") each month, when galleries open their doors in the evenings and artists who are not currently exhibiting bring their wares to the sidewalks.

Here are a few galleries that have withstood the test of time.

The **Alysia Duckler Gallery** (922 NW 11th Avenue, Portland, 503-223-7595, www.alysiaducklergallery.com) features the works of such artists as Trude Parkinson and Esther Podemski. Photography, drawings, and paintings are the major focus.

The **Lawrence Gallery** (903 NW Davis Street, The Pearl, 503-228-1776, www.lawrencegallery.net) is nationally known for its stunning presentation of artworks in a wide variety of media — paintings, jewelry, sculpture, clay, and wood are all represented, in formats varying from realistic to abstract.

For folk arts and handicrafts, try **The Real Mother Goose** (901 SW Yamhill Street, Downtown, 503-223-9510, www.therealmothergoose .com), which topped *NICHE* magazine's poll of America's top craft galleries two years in a row. The gallery showcases artists from all over the Pacific Northwest.

The **Augen Gallery** (817 SW 2nd Avenue, Downtown, 503-224-8182; and 716 NW Davis Street, 503-546-5056; www.augengallery.com) features works by contemporary Northwest artists, as well as prints and works on paper by artists from beyond the region.

Blue Sky Gallery (122 NW 8th Avenue, 503-225-0210, www.bluesky gallery.org) is one of the oldest member-supported, non-profit photographic art spaces in the country. It is always on the cutting edge.

Founded in 1990 as an artist collective, **Gallery 114** (1100 NW Glisan Street, The Pearl, 503-243-3356, gallery114.org) and its members have consistently presented the city with an ever-changing diversity of artwork.

Quintana Galleries (120 NW 9th Avenue, Downtown, 503-223-1729, www.quintanagalleries.com) is one of the nation's most important galleries for native art and represents some of the finest contemporary Northwest Coast native artists.

S E C R E T

GARDENS

The least you would expect from the City of Roses is a generous number of gardens. You will not be disappointed. You'll find rose gardens, rhododendron gardens, rock gardens, botanical gardens, and herb gardens, just to mention a few.

The **International Rose Test Garden** (400 SW Kingston Avenue, Washington Park, 503-227-7033, www.rosegardenstore.org) is a meticulously tended 4.5-acre plot of exotic roses that includes Climbing Ophelia, Sweet Juliet, and, yes, Elizabeth Taylor. Begun in 1917, it's the oldest test garden in the country. Spread grandly over a ridge, the garden offers a breathtaking panoramic view of the city. If people have been nagging you to stop and smell the roses, come here to breathe in the fragrance of more than 8,000 flowers from 550 varieties.

Do you think there is very little left to be discovered in this world? The **Leach Botanical Garden** (6704 SE 122nd Avenue, Gilbert, 503-823-9503, www.leachgarden.org) will prove you wrong. Lilla Leach, an accomplished botanist, discovered five plant species new to science right in the property they called "Sleepy Hollow." Today, the Leach Botanical Garden occupies a woodland area carved by

Johnson Creek in southeast Portland. There are no tidy gravel paths or geometric designs in this garden. Instead, you'll walk among towering firs, lush shrubbery, and fantastic flowers. The garden, devoted to both the Leach Collection and Northwest native plants, is an urban oasis.

The **Portland Classical Chinese Garden** (NW 3rd Avenue and Everett Street, Old Town Chinatown, 503-228-8131, www.portland chinesegarden.com) is an authentic Suzhou-style garden. It has grown out of the friendship between Portland and its sister city of Suzhou, a metropolis known for its exquisite gardens. Tall buildings ring this intricate delight, which was brought over, volcanic rock by volcanic rock, from China and assembled by Chinese artisans. The pagoda-roofed buildings are elaborately carved, and a waterfall and pond provide the appropriate *feng shui*. An elegant dark-wood teahouse is the perfect place to sip a cup of green tea.

Even the government loves gardening in Portland. A beautiful little roof garden adorns the ninth floor of the **Federal Courthouse** (1000 SW 3rd Avenue, Downtown). It's open to the public, although you will have to undergo a security check to enter the building. The garden has lots of whimsical art pieces and a fountain, as well as great views of the Willamette River and downtown Portland.

The **Berry Botanic Garden** (11505 SW Summerville Avenue, Riverdale, 503-636-4112, www.berrybot.org), nestled in the hills of southwest Portland, spreads out over almost seven acres. Founded in 1977, it has a collection of rhododendrons, alpine flowers, and unusual perennials. Volunteers maintain most of the garden, and there are always opportunities for ivy removers, seed germinators, and greenhouse volunteers.

The **Hulda Klager Lilac Gardens** (115 South Pekin Road, Woodland, Washington, 360-225-8996, www.lilacgardens.com), not far

from the city, feature a charming Victorian farmhouse and a garden dedicated to lilacs. You can wander the grounds, which include the house, a woodshed, a water tower, a windmill, and the gardens — all restored by the volunteer Hulda Klager Lilac Society. Who was Hulda Klager? An avid gardener who hybridized lilacs. Not surprisingly, the best time to see this garden is in the spring.

Finally, did you know that there are 101 varieties of camellias on the University of Portland campus? If you start now, you just may find all of them.

SECRET
GAS JOCKEYS

Remember those days when "you could trust your car to the men who wear the star?"

Well, perhaps you're too young. But there was a time when you drove your auto into a gas station and, lo and behold, someone appeared at your window to ask, "Fill 'er up?"

I'm happy to tell you those days still exist in Portland. In fact, it's illegal to pump your own gas in Oregon. Don't worry about a couple of extra cents per gallon — after all, you're not paying any sales tax. Relax. Enjoy the experience of having someone else fill your tank in all kinds of weather.

SECRET

GEOLOGY

Ride the Westside MAX line to the Washington Park stop to see the geological timeline exhibit that decorates the walls of this 260-foot-deep train stop — the deepest underground transit stop in North America. Elevators take a mere 20 seconds to whisk you to the surface. At the aboveground entrance to the transit plaza, there's a sculpture made from columnar basalt and etched granite that tells the story of the light-rail tunnel's creation.

SECRET

GOVERNOR

Anglers of all ages should tip their hats to former governor Tom Mc-Call. His concern for the environment was legendary. It's thanks to him that you can go downtown in Portland, toss a line into the river, catch a salmon, and feel safe having it for dinner.

Tom McCall first came onto the Portland scene as a journalist and television commentator. From there he moved into politics, which eventually took him to the governor's office.

Some of his critics say that he took his concern for the environment too far and it hurt the state economy. But it was the '60s, and Tom McCall's concerns largely reflected those of his constituents. Yes, this is the same governor who told people to come and visit but not to stay. At the time, no one took him to task — not until the economy took a downturn.

His unpopular moves have long been overshadowed by his achievements during his two terms in office. One of those successes was cleaning up the Willamette River. That feat got him national attention, and other cities looked to Portland as an example. It is extremely fitting that Portland's newest waterfront park has been named in his honor.

S E C R E T

GROTTO
❧

The Grotto (NE 85th Avenue and Sandy Boulevard, Roseway, 503-254-7371, www.thegrotto.org), more properly known as the Sanctuary of Our Sorrowful Mother, is run by the Friars of the Order of the Servants of Mary (Servites). Don't let the slightly tacky strip mall ambiance of Sandy Boulevard prevent you from entering The Grotto. This internationally renowned Catholic sanctuary is an oasis of solitude and peace, despite the almost 150,000 visitors who wander through the grounds each year. A rock cave carved into the base of a 110-foot cliff features a replica of Michelangelo's famous *Pieta* in its center. The Grotto is spread over several levels. The central plaza is lush with firs and rhododendrons that lead you to the heart of the sanctuary, Our Lady's Grotto. Another level features a chapel and a gift shop. But you must ride the elevator (there is a charge) to the top to see the magnificent view of the Columbia River Valley, the Cascade Range, and what remains of Mount St. Helens. Particularly impressive is the 180-degree floor-to-ceiling view through the beveled glass wall of the Meditation Chapel.

SECRET

HAPPY HOURS

Don't look for signs proclaiming "happy hour." The puritanical Oregon Liquor Control Commission has seen fit to ban the advertising of such — be it known as happy hour, social adjustment hour, no rush hour, twilight time, or even pirate time. But this doesn't mean that you can't find a good drink with munchies at the right time for the right price.

Suki's Steak House (2401 sw 4th Avenue, Downtown, 503-226-1181) has $2 well drinks, and $2.50 brews with *gratis* appetizers such as wings and mini tacos. Play a free round of pool, and you might even work up an appetite for one of Suki's steaks.

Bluehour (250 NW 13th Avenue, Downtown, 503-226-3394, www .bluehouronline.com) is a chic and sleek place to head for happy hour. The café and bar can be an audio challenge when full, but the food deals are fabulous, affordable, and interesting — this may be the only place in the city where you can nibble on fried olives.

SECRET

HARDWARE

Most visitors don't come to a city with hardware on their minds. Let Portland revise your thinking. **Rejuvenation Hardware** (1100 SE Grand Avenue, Buckman, 503-238-1900, www.rejuvenation.com) has two floors of cool stuff for people with a passion for their homes. On the fringe of the Hawthorne District, it features reproduction lighting, along with architectural secondhand bits, such as doors, windows, and lots of old molding. There are also items for bathrooms, kitchens, drawers, and closets.

The **1874 House** (8070 SE 13th Avenue, Downtown, 503-233-1874) is filled with old plumbing materials, stained glass, moldings, and other trimmings to make your historic home the showplace you desire. Or you can simply pick up something neat to add a dash of yesterday to your modern abode.

S E C R E T

HAWAIIAN

Noho's Hawaiian Café (2525 SE Clinton Street, Hosford-Abernethy, 503-233-5301, www.nohos.com) is the place to put away some serious food. If you've experienced a "two-scoop" plate lunch while on vacation in Hawaii, you'll understand the generous helpings of macaroni and rice salads. Yakisoba, Korean ribs, and ono chicken are just a few of the menu offerings. The place is usually packed, so be prepared to wait a while or consider take-out.

SECRET

HIKES

Ah, fresh air! Mother Nature! Trails to wander! Okay, you've been sedentary for too long, and now you just can't resist the call of the forested path. Not to fear — Portland has paths for the amateur, the professional, and everyone in between.

Oak Island Nature Loop (Sauvie Island Wildlife Area, 18330 NW Sauvie Island Road, 503-621-3488, sauvieisland.org) is an easy, almost flat loop smack in the middle of the Sauvie Island Wildlife Area. This pleasant amble offers views of blue herons and, in the distance, Mount St. Helens and Mount Adams. It will cost you $3.50 for a parking permit, but that's a small price to pay for serenity.

The seven-mile **McNeil Point hike** (Mount Hood National Forest, 503-622-4822 or 888-622-4822, www.mthood.info) will reward your uphill efforts with magnificent vistas of the Cascade Range, glacier-fed ponds, and alpine meadows. Try this only if you are really in shape. Seven miles is a long, long hike. You will need a $5 Northwest Forest Pass for the day.

Closer to the city is **Forest Park**, a 5,100-acre urban forest that lies close to the core and has an extensive network of almost 70 miles of trails in its tree-covered expanse.

And, if you like your wetlands curbside head to **Tanner Springs Park** (NW 10th Avenue at Marshall Street, The Pearl) for a glimpse of how renovation can truly revive parts of a city. This pocket-size park was returned to its estuarial roots by allowing its underground waters to once again flow. Not much of a hike, but great for inner-city serenity and bird-watching.

SECRET

HISTORY

An eight-story *trompe l'oeil* mural welcomes you as you enter the brick courtyard of the **Oregon History Center** (1200 sw Park Avenue, Downtown, 503-222-1741, www.ohs.org), one of the landmark buildings in the South Park Blocks cultural district. The center houses a museum, archives, research library, and — most importantly for many tourists — a shop, all of which are open to the public. This is the place to find *the* penny used in the actual coin toss that determined the name of the city (see "Secret Penny"). Native American artifacts and a multimedia exploration of Portland's light-rail system are just a few of the highlights.

The **End of the Oregon Trail Interpretive Center** (1726 Washington Street, Oregon City, Oregon, 503-657-9336) houses a mixed-media dramatization of what life was like over 150 years ago. Costumed interpreters — I have always wanted to be one of them —- teach an easy version of Oregon Trail 101. There are exhibits of artifacts and heirlooms left behind by those who undertook this arduous journey.

The center was built in 1995 on the former Donation Land Claim of George Abernethy, the first elected governor of the Oregon Country. A merchant and miller by trade, Abernethy had a vested interest in the continued growth of Oregon City. So he allowed new immigrants to park their wagons, graze their oxen, and set up camp on a meadow behind his home. That meadow came to be known as Abernethy Green, and for many of the early Oregon Trail pioneers, it truly was the trail's end.

If you plan to follow in the footsteps of many of these early migrants, you can get trail maps at the interpretive center. Both rut nuts and novices will find guidebooks and maps to suit their interests. If you can't make it to the center, you can ask staff to send you a map by e-mail or snail mail.

Aside from being the official end of the Oregon Trail, Oregon City also lays claim to many significant firsts — the first public library west of the Rockies (1842), the first incorporated city west of the Rockies (1844), and the first navigational locks in the Northwest (1873).

If you haven't satisfied your curiosity about life in 19th-century Oregon, then you should head directly to the **Fort Vancouver National Historic Site** (612 E Reserve Street, Vancouver, Washington, 360-816-6230). Yes, you will have to cross the river into a different state, but the trip is worth the not-too-long trek.

First the headquarters of the Hudson's Bay Company's Columbia-region trade (1825–49), then a U.S. military post until 1860, it has been reconstructed to reflect its days as an army post. The grand officers' quarters along Officers' Row have all been restored. The Marshall House, named for commanding officer George C. Marshall, is the fort's showpiece, and has been fully furnished with antiques of the period. The fort's historic 1840s gardens continue to flourish; some consider them the seedbeds of Northwest horticulture and agriculture. The English-style gardens are the first known local planting of vegetables, herbs, and flowers in a formal plot. The original gardener was Billy Bruce, who learned his craft from the Royal Horticultural Society on the Duke of Devonshire's estates.

SECRET

HOOPS

Psst. Wanna shoot some hoops in a volcano? At **Mount Tabor Park** (SE 60th Street and Salmon Street, Mount Tabor), you can play some b-ball within the cone of an extinct volcano atop this cool, forested park. And when your game is over, enjoy a hike through the woods; if you hike to the top, you'll be rewarded with truly beautiful views of downtown Portland to the west and Mount Hood to the east.

If you want to play indoors, try the **Beaverton Hoop YMCA** (9685 SW Harvest Court, Beaverton, Oregon, 503-644-2191, www.thehoop. com). The facility has lots of courts, as well as other workout facilities, including weights and aerobic equipment. You'll have to pony up $25 for a one-week pass, but it's a good deal. If you want to play, call first for times and costs.

SECRET

IMPERSONATORS

Darcelle XV Showplace (208 NW 3rd Avenue, 503-222-5338, www .darcellexv.com) is home to the most famous drag show in Portland. (Just how many could there be in a city this size?) Located in the slightly funky Old Town Chinatown part of Portland, it entertains audiences with impersonators, strippers, and even a Chippendale-style chorus line. It's glitz, glamour, and comedy. Go all out and catch the dinner show, which includes a free limo ride to the club.

SECRET

INDIAN

Take the MAX train to **India House** (1038 SW Morrison Street, Downtown, 503-274-1017, www.indiahouseportland.com), because you'll want to freely sample the Indian beer along with your food. At this basic, yet elegant, restaurant, you can choose how hot or mild you wish your dish. The naan and vegetarian dishes are the highlights of the menu. Be sure to nibble on some seasoned anise seeds at the end of your meal. They're the Indian equivalent of parsley to sweeten your breath.

SECRET

IRISH

In **Biddy McGraw's** (6000 NE Glisan Street, Laurelhurst, 503-233-1178, www.biddymcgraws.com), you'll hear half the patrons using an honest-to-sod, shipped-over-from-the-land-of-green accent. It's not just the accents that make Biddy McGraw's authentic — it's the political overtones. Posters on the wall urge "all-party peace talks," among other sentiments. Guinness is on tap, as well as other drafts and ciders. The dance floor is suitably large for the heel-kicking Celtic tunes, and on Sunday nights there's a three-course dinner straight from the old country.

On St. Patrick's Day, the place to be is **Kells Irish Restaurant and Pub** (112 SW 2nd Avenue, Downtown, 503-227-4057, WWW

.kellsirish.com). The Guinness is on tap, of course. The whiskey selection is staggering — or, at least, it will have you staggering if you try to work your way through the list. Got money to throw away? Ask your waiter to stick a dollar bill to the ceiling (don't ask how it works — it's a secret), and you can go on your way with the knowledge that your money will end up at a deserving charity. There's live music, usually Irish, every night of the week, beginning around 9 PM.

SECRET
ISLAND

When you feel the need for wide-open empty space, drive to Portland's nearby pastoral oasis — **Sauvie Island** (Route 30, west to the Sauvie Island Bridge, www.sauvieisland.org). The island is a popular Portland getaway, but you almost never feel overrun with fellow human beings because of its generous size. You'll discover relatively isolated beaches — including one that's clothing optional — and numerous hiking trails that meander through wetlands, pastures, oak woodlands, and coniferous forests. More stretches of sandy beach can be found on Oak Island, a much smaller land mass connected to the northeast end of Sauvie by a natural bridge. This is also where you will find a seasonal corn maze.

Sauvie Island is much, much more than just a recreational retreat. Here, vegetable gardens, berry fields, and orchards stretch for miles. If you feel the urge, join the throngs who come to pick their own.

The **Sauvie Island Wildlife Area** (18330 NW Sauvie Island Road,

503-621-3488), a 20-square mile refuge for waterfowl, covers much of the north end of the island. Make sure to ask at the refuge headquarters, about two miles north of the Sauvie Island Bridge, for a map and bird-watching advice.

Tip: Gasoline is not available on the island, so make sure you have enough for your return trip.

S E C R E T

ITALIAN

Caffe Mingo (807 NW 21st Avenue, Northwest, 503-226-4646) is a tiny restaurant with an exposed kitchen and dim lighting that will make you think you are having dinner in an Italian farmhouse. Cans of olive oil and blocks of Parmesan complete the Tuscan atmosphere. You could make a meal of salad, bread, and wine. But why? The pastas are plentiful and the tiramisu cheesecake is divinely decadent.

The Hotel Vintage Plaza is home to **Pazzo Ristorante** (627 SW Washington Street, Downtown, 503-228-1515, www.pazzo.com). A wood-burning pizza oven dominates the dining room, giving the room a high-energy feeling. This is more than just your average Italian restaurant. There are monthly wine tastings, regional tasting evenings, and cooking classes where you can work one-on-one with the chef in the main kitchen.

Rustica Italian Cafe (1700 NE Broadway, Sullivan's Gulch, 503-288-0990) features classic Italian dishes and an extensive wine list. The antipasti is delicioso and you'll have your hands full just deciding on which of the pastas to sample. The atmosphere is casual and comfortable. A good place when you want Italian with no surprises.

Alba Osteria & Enoteca (6440 sw Capitol Highway, 503-977-3045, www.albaosteria.com), tucked away in the spiffy Hillsdale neighborhood, is a bright and convivial gathering spot that serves up classic Italian dishes with an American touch. What's really fun about Alba Osteria & Enoteca — aside from the items on the menu — is the choice of dining rooms, which are lined up like boxcars. If you don't like the ambiance in one area, go for a stroll until you find a table that suits your mood.

Are you tired of fast food? Then try **Serrato** (2112 nw Kearney Street, Northwest, 503-221-1195, www.serratto.com) for a pure definition of slow food. Slow food? That's a meal that unfolds before you one course at a time — food to be savored, not wolfed down at lightning speed. The first-rate Italian fare extends well beyond the marinara sauce of the average pasta emporium. Start with a simple plate of mozzarella, tomatoes, basil, and bread. Follow that with an entrée of fish or a filled pasta, such as agnolotti. If you still have room, try a dessert, maybe panna cotta decorated with blueberries.

Looking for just the right combination of romantic and affordable? Take your squeeze to **Ristorante Fratelli** (1230 nw Hoyt Street, The Pearl, 503-241-8800, www.fratellicucina.com) for candlelight, a wood-burning fireplace, and a menu that goes beyond just red sauce on spaghetti. The service is attentive, but not so much that it will interfere with any special moments.

Once upon a time, **Martinotti's** (404 sw 10th Avenue, Downtown, 503-224-9028) was the only place in Portland where you could find Italian olive oil, sun-dried tomatoes, and other assorted goodies. Although many places in the city now sell these ingredients, Martinotti's still is the place to shop. Go just to inhale all the delicious aromas or to seek the advice of some of the Martinotti family members. See Armand for wines — his nose knows.

3 Doors Down Café (1429 SE 37th Avenue, Sunnyside, 503-236-6886, www.3doorsdowncafe.com) makes the kind of hearty, homespun fare your Italian-American mother might make, if you had an Italian-American mother. Good breads, topped with cannellini bean spread. Caramelized caponata made gorgeous with Gorgonzola. Penne with a sweet, creamy tomato and vodka sauce. The menu changes every two weeks, so you can go again, and again, and again. Did I tell you about the tiramisu? It's possibly the best in Portland. Reservations are not accepted.

SECRET

JAPANESE

Are you looking for a vintage Naugahyde banquette on which to rest your buns while you scarf down sushi? Look no further than **Saburo** (1667 SE Bybee Boulevard, Sellwood-Moreland, 503-236-4237, www.saburos.com), a shoebox-sized eatery with a loyal clientele. Expect a long wait for possibly the freshest, most generous portions of sushi in Portland, at a fair price. Saburo is the closest you'll come in this city to a neighborhood Japanese restaurant.

If your heart desires a more upscale Japanese experience head to **Biwa** (215 SE 9th Avenue, Buckman, 503-239-8830, www.biwarestaurant.com) to sip sake and nibble on such goodies as Korean beef tartare, yakimono, or a delicate radish salad. More substantial fare includes bowls of udon noodles and barbecued pork.

Can't afford a trip to the land of the rising sun? Then escape to the **Japanese Garden** (611 sw Kingston Avenue, Washington Park, 503-223-1321, www.japanesegarden.com). Five traditional gardens and a ceremonial teahouse on a hillside provide an authentic experience. The Japanese ambassador to the United States pronounced this the most beautiful garden outside Japan. In the spring, flowering cherry trees and azaleas accent the grounds; in the summer, irises abound; and in the fall, maples blaze with bright oranges and reds. Does this mean you shouldn't visit in the winter? Not at all. The gardens' spare serenity provides a Zen tranquility in which to wander.

Even Governor Tom McCall Waterfront Park has an Asian flavor. Beyond the Waterfront Story Garden, you will find a walkway that passes 100 Japanese cherry trees in the **Japanese-American Historical Plaza**, which honors the Japanese-Americans interned during World War II. Memorable quotes by Oregonians who were interned are set in boulders along the pathway. To the north, at the foot of the Steel Bridge, you will find the *Friendship Circle*, a sculpture that emits the sound of a Japanese flute and drum. The circle was created to honor the friendship between Portland and Sapporo, Japan, another of Portland's sister cities.

For all things Japanese, such as nori, pickled ginger, and octopus, head for **Anzen Hiroshi's Inc.** (736 NE Martin Luther King Jr. Boulevard, Kerns, 503-233-5111). This emporium is crammed full of all things Japanese — lacquerware, books, magazines, and lots and lots of food, including food to go. You can pick up a bento box and head to an Asian garden for a picnic.

Drive up Sandy Boulevard and follow your nose to **Du's Grill** (5365 NE Sandy Boulevard, Hollywood, 503-284-1773). The humble exterior belies the magic within. Meat is prepared over an open flame in both Japanese and Korean fashions. Hint: Du's may be the only place in town that offers Korean "fast" food.

Uwajimaya (10500 sw Beaverton–Hillsdale Highway, 503-643-4512, www.uwajimaya.com) means "heaven," and so it is to the shopper in need of Asian goods. It's a full-sized supermarket crammed to the rafters with all kinds of Asian specialties. Need lemongrass? Look no further. A book in Japanese? The Kinokuniya bookstore chain has a branch on the premises. The offerings are primarily Japanese, but you will also find Chinese and other Asian goodies onsite.

A small museum in the heart of what was once Portland's Japantown pays tribute to the contributions of the Japanese in Oregon. The **Oregon Nikkei Legacy Center** (121 NW 2nd Avenue, Old Town Chinatown, 503-224-1458, www.oregonnikkei.org) chronicles the arrival of the first Issei in Oregon in the 1880s, the thriving communities of the 1930s, Japanese-Americans' displacement to internment camps during World War II, and postwar resettlement. Who knew there was once a Nisei Baseball League?

And then there is tea. Among Portland's well-respected tea schools is **Wakai Dokokai** (contact Louise Bowman at 503-228-7957 or 503-242-1557, www.wakaitea.org), where students learn about Japanese tea culture and the "way of tea." Classes are ongoing, but on the last Tuesday of every month, instructors invite visitors to take part in an elaborate Japanese tea ceremony. Join other guests in discovering respect, purity, harmony, and tranquility in a bowl of green tea. Cost is about $10 and the ceremony lasts approximately two hours.

Round up a group of friends, convince one of them to be your designated driver and head to Forest Grove (about 30 minutes west of Portland) and tingle your tastebuds with some sake tasting. **SakeOne**

(820 Elm Street, Forest Grove, 503-357-7056, www.sakeone.com) is the only American-owned sake distillery in the United States, and the only certified organic sake carrying the USDA organic seal. But, the tasting part is an adventure because SakeOne makes fruit- and herb-infused specialty sakes. Open daily from 11AM–5PM.

SECRET
JAZZ

The **Lobby Court** (Benson Hotel, 309 sw Broadway, Downtown, 503-228-2000, www.bensonhotel.com) is hands-down the most elegant bar in the city. The old-world ambiance and gentle jazz playing in the background set the mood for sipping a martini or Scotch. Tuesdays through Saturdays, you'll hear live music.

And then there's **Jimmy Mak's** (221 NW 10th Avenue, The Pearl, 503-295-6542, www.jimmymaks.com), with all the ambiance of a convention banquet room in a cheap hotel. Ignore the ambiance, or lack of it; it's the music you've come to hear. Some of the best jazz bands in town play here. The place is at least comfortable, with a full bar and menu.

The **Mt. Hood Jazz Festival** (www.mthoodjazz.org) is the grand-daddy of the music festivals in the Rose City. Most frequently held on the grounds of Mt. Hood Community College in Gresham, just a few minutes northeast of the downtown core, this volunteer-run festival attracts top-level performers to its events spread over a two-week period in the summer.

If you like your jazz cool, then the February **Portland Jazz Festival** (www.pdxjazz.com) is for you, daddy-o. This event features over 125 acts, many of them Grammy winners, held at various venues around the city.

SECRET
JEWELRY
❖

For more than a century, locals and visitors have been buying and window shopping at **Dan Marx** (511 sw Broadway, Downtown, 503-228-5090), Oregon's oldest jewelry store. The staff has a quiet, almost reverential demeanor — good jewelry is serious business. This little family-owned shop is filled with small and delicate treasures.

Carl Greve (640 sw Broadway, 503-223-7121, www.carlgreve.com) is a favorite store of brides-to-be. They climb the starry staircase (I'm not kidding) to a second floor filled with shimmering china, glassware, and accessories. The lines represented here are almost as exclusive as the jewelry one floor down.

Carl Brockman, the owner of **Goldmark** (1000 sw Taylor Street, Downtown, 503-224-3743), loves to work with customers to create one-of-a-kind pieces of jewelry by restyling and updating older pieces. Carl has been fascinated with this profession for more than 25 years and has turned out some incredible creations from old jewelry.

SECRET

KARAOKE

Mondays to Saturdays, one of the most popular karaoke spots is **Bush Garden** (900 sw Morrison Street, Downtown, 503-226-7181, www.bush-garden.com). This seemingly serene Japanese restaurant shakes off its Dr. Jekyll personality at night and rocks. Asian businessmen, college students, and rock 'n' roll wannabes take turns at the microphone. It's even more fun if you sip a sake while you take in the music.

Chopsticks Express (2651 E Burnside Street, Kerns, 503-234-6171) has a down-on-its-heels lounge in the back of its fast food emporium that has become *the* rock 'n' roll karaoke hot spot. Dive on in and belt out a tune.

SECRET

KISSES

Possibly the most secret, and romantic, place to kiss in downtown Portland is behind the waterfall at the **Ira C. Keller Memorial Fountain**. Facing the Keller Auditorium, this fountain has two levels. The top level is made up of brooks that run through a tree-shaded plaza. The brooks taper down and overflow to create a waterfall. If you don't mind getting a little wet, you can smooch on the bench just behind the waterfall.

SECRET
LIBRARIES

Books. Of course, you'll find books in the **Multnomah County Central Library** (801 sw 10th Avenue, Downtown, 503-988-5123). You'll also find a Starbucks (reading is thirsty work) and one of the best stores for book lovers. **The Friends Library Store** (503-445-4903, www.friends-library.org) is a tiny nook filled with bookends, book lights, writing implements, jewelry, children's gifts, and lots of books, books, books.

At the same branch, the **Beverly Cleary Children's Library** (503-248-5123) is a literary moppet's delight, with approximately 50,000 books. An impressive bronze tree with castings of animals supports the librarian's desk. Shadow boxes make up three large bookends, and there are 16 computers. Cleary, the popular author of many children's books, grew up in northeast Portland and once worked in the children's library.

The **Heathman Hotel** (1001 sw Broadway, Downtown, 503-241-4100 or 800-551-0011, portland.heathmanhotel.com, see "Secret Luxury") has a secret treasure: signed copies of books by authors who have spent the night in the hotel. Also stashed in the Heathman Hotel is a secret video library — and not just a skimpy choice of half a dozen movies no one in their right mind would want to see, but an 18-page listing of more than 250 movies, including classic, art, and independent films. Of course, you do have to stay in the hotel to use the library.

SECRET

LIFTS

꙳

Life already has its ups and downs, so you may not be looking for any more of those, but there are a few places in the Portland area that can give you quite a lift. Inside **Powell's City of Books** (1005 W Burnside Street, The Pearl, 503-228-4651, see "Secret Books"), you'll find the world's only three-door elevator. It's just another one of the whimsical touches that makes Portland, well, Portland.

Just outside Portland, in Oregon City, is one of my favorite elevators. As Oregon City grew, it became tiring to get from the lower level of town to the new upper level, along the bluffs. Until the first stairs were built in the mid-1860s, folks used old trails to climb up. In 1912, city commissioners asked voters to approve a bond measure to construct and operate an elevator from the lower part of town to the upper part. The measure failed when first put to a vote in July, but it passed in a second referendum held in December. Originally, the elevator was powered by water, resulting in a three-minute ride. In 1924, the power source was changed to electricity, and the ride was reduced to a rapid 30 seconds. The lower entrance is at 7th Street and Railroad Avenue, and the upper is at S High Street, near 7th Street.

SECRET

LINKS

In general, I subscribe to Mark Twain's opinion that "golf is a good walk spoiled." But there are those who like to chase a small ball over hill and dale, and Portland has some pretty good places to do just that.

The **Rose City Golf Course** (2200 NE 71st Avenue, Roseway, 503-253-4744) is the place for those who like a challenge. One of many municipal courses, Rose City is tricky because of its many trees. Hills add a few more challenges, and most of the holes sport bunkers. Just to add to the fun, the rye grass fairway can be soggy, like a lot of the courses in Portland.

The **Pumpkin Ridge Golf Club** (12930 Old Pumpkin Ridge Road, North Plains, Oregon, 503-647-4747, www.pumpkinridge. com) has two courses. The Ghost Creek course is a superb semi-private experience. The greens are not overly fast and provide a true roll. You'll also enjoy the change in layout from the front nine to the back nine, as trees and tight fairways give way to a more open, links-style course. On the private course, Witch Hollow, Tiger Woods became the first golfer to win three consecutive US Amateur Championship titles.

At **Heron Lakes Golf Course** (3500 N Victory Boulevard, Bridgeton, 503-289-1818, www.heronlakesgolf.com), you can do some birdwatching along with your golfing. There are two courses. The Greenback has more trees and a more typical Northwest layout. The Great Blue is a traditional links-style course, with mounds full of jungle-tall, ball-hungry grasses. Don't be surprised to encounter several of the giant birds for which the course is named. And that swarm of bees you think you hear in the background? That's just the boys at the Portland Speedway playing with their toys.

My favorite course is **The Pub Course at Edgefield** (2126 sw Halsey Street, Troutdale, Oregon, 503-669-8610). When a golf course is designed, the natural terrain is usually bulldozed, leveled, built back up, and sculptured meticulously to reflect the creator's vision. But the McMenamin brothers (see "Secret Brothers") are not noted for doing the usual. When putting an 18-hole pitch-and-putt course around their Edgefield resort, they decided to retain the natural lay of the land. Ahem. It makes things interesting and at times, difficult. But you always know there's a cool glass of something waiting for you at the end.

It's not a hard course; there were six holes-in-one within two weeks of the course's opening (none were mine). But what else would you expect from these boys, since their philosophy is that things don't have to be straight to be fun?

SECRET
LODGING

Ever want to stay where a rock star would feel at home? Ace is the place. The **Ace Hotel** (1022 sw Stark Street, Downtown, 503-228-2277, www.acehotel.com) puts a whole new spin on downtown lodging. Built in an historic 1912 building, the hotel has furnished the rooms and lobby with as many recycled and upcycled pieces as possible, from the reception "desk" to the wifi-friendly lounge. Rooms range in rate from under $100 to over $250, some have shared baths, and some feature claw-footed bathtubs. The location is certainly a bonus, on the edge of the Pearl, close to Powells' Books, and with a Kenny and Zuke's deli next door, you really couldn't ask for more. But there is more, including it being pet and family friendly, and it having turntables and vinyl in some rooms, laundry facilities available, and complimentary computer access.

SECRET

LUST
❦

Need a little lust in your life? Head for **Spartacus** (300 SW 12th Avenue, Downtown, 503-224-2604, spartacusstore.com) to load up on lingerie for women and men, love potions, oils, and interesting toys. The lingerie selection is a little more S&M than dainty. The **Fantasy Land Two** (16014 SE 82nd Drive, Clackamas, Oregon, 503-655-4667) stocks more than most people could imagine in their hottest fantasies. Go with someone you love, or are at least in lust with, to enjoy a wicked afternoon or evening of shopping.

SECRET

LUXURY
❦

If it's time for you to splurge on accommodation, Portland does not lack places where you can pretend you have just won the lottery. In many cases, the hotels are in renovated older buildings whose owners have managed to retain the charm of years gone by.

The **Benson** (309 sw Broadway, Downtown, 503-228-2000 or 888-5BENSON, www.bensonhotel.com) is old Portland, opulent and luxurious. Philanthropist and lumber baron Simon Benson — the same Benson who provided the city with its Benson bubbler water fountains — saw the need for an outstanding hotel in the growing city. Completed in 1912, it is graced by Austrian crystal chandeliers, Circassian walnut walls, and Italian marble floors. The rooms are a bit small and the service is a tad on the corporate side (distant and disinterested). It is, however, conveniently located in the heart of the city.

The **Heathman Hotel** (1001 sw Broadway, Downtown, 503-241-4100 or 800-551-0011, portland.heathmanhotel.com) is one of the city's finest and prides itself on the lengths it will go to satisfy a client. It is said that when Pavarotti came to stay, the Heathman prevailed upon the city to stop daytime construction so that the tenor could rest before his performance. It's a beautiful, grande dame of a hotel, with cushy chairs and bold, modern artworks. The President stays here when he comes to town.

RiverPlace (1510 sw Harbor Way, Downtown, 503-228-3233 or 800-227-1333, www.riverplacehotel.com) is the city's only waterfront resort. This European-style hotel (small, elegant, personal) overlooks the marina and RiverPlace neighborhood. With fewer than 100 rooms, all endowed with wingback chairs and overstuffed sofas, RiverPlace is more like a posh home than a hotel. What else makes it so Euro? Continental breakfasts, shoeshines, and concierge services. It's a great place to watch the annual Christmas Boat Parade along the Willamette.

You don't have to be a governor, or even a mayor, to stay at **The Governor Hotel** (614 sw 11th Avenue, Downtown, 503-224-3400 or 800-554-3456, www.governorhotel.com). The guest rooms, all 100 of them, vary slightly in décor. So if you stay more than once, each time will be a delightful surprise. Fascinating hand-painted murals throughout the public areas pay tribute to Lewis and Clark and the Native Americans they encountered while exploring the Oregon Territory. Guests of the quietly elegant hotel can use the full-service athletic club, which includes a lap pool, whirlpool, track, and weight room.

SECRET

MANSION

Wouldn't you love to live in a mansion — a grand, glorious, gingerbread-trimmed house such as the **Pittock Mansion** (3229 nw Pittock Drive, Washington Park, 503-823-3623 or 503-823-3624, pittockmansion.org)? Henry and Georgina Pittock created this stately, 16,000-square-foot home, built in 1914. The 22 rooms, furnished with antiques, include an oval parlor and a smoking room. You can't live or stay overnight in the mansion, but you can picnic on the grounds and enjoy a sweeping vista of mountains, rivers, and the city. Roses, azaleas, and rhododendrons flourish on the property. It will make you wish you had brought your parasol and very best beau.

SECRET

MARKETS

One of the best-kept secrets for travelers is the **Portland Farmers Market** (Saturdays, May through October, on the campus of Portland State University, Downtown, www.portlandfarmersmarket. org). The market highlights local growers and harvesters, and features fresh flowers, seafood, breads, nuts, produce, and locally prepared foods. On Wednesdays, the market moves a little closer to the downtown core, setting up shop in the South Park Blocks, near the Portland Center for Performing Arts. The market hosts several special events, including the Summer Loaf Festival, the Great Pumpkin Event, and Tomatofest.

The market has proved so popular with residents that a special edition now operates on Thursday nights during the season at the campus location. It's a terrific addition for travelers who would like to pretend they're touring a European city and have no time to stop for dinner. Just pick up a baguette, some cheese, and fruit, and continue on your way. The **PSU Market** (South Park blocks between sw Harrison Street and sw Montgomery Street) is a lively market with a young college vibe. Don't even think about driving here: take the Max or the Streetcar that will drop you just steps away from the fun.

The **Eastbank Market** (se 20th at Salmon between se Belmont Street and se Hawthorne Street, Buckman) is open on Thursdays during the summer, from mid-afternoon to early evening. Perfect for picking up ingredients after work or while enroute to a friends.

The **Ecotrust Market** (located in the parking lot of the Jean Vollum Natural Capital Center on NW 10th between NW Irving Street and NW Johnson Street) is the Pearl district's solution to a farmers market. After all, you can walk all day in stilettos but sometime you have to eat.

SECRET
MARY JANE
❀

Oregon was the first US state to regulate marijuana for medical use, issuing registration cards to anyone who has cancer, glaucoma, an HIV-related disease, severe muscle wasting, pain, nausea, seizures, or muscle spasms, and to people whose doctors agree that marijuana might alleviate their symptoms. Nobody looks forward to dreaded diseases or old age, but I do like the human approach this state brings to medical care. Jeannelle Bluhm, who has multiple sclerosis, received the first such license in 1999. She told a reporter from the *Oregonian* that she had plans to home-can some tomatoes and preserve some marijuana in sandwich bags.

SECRET
MAYOR
❀

J.E. "Bud" Clark served as Portland's controversial and flamboyant mayor from 1984 to 1992. During his term in office, he oversaw the development of Pioneer Courthouse Square and Pioneer Place. A longtime Portland resident, Clark embodied civic activism: among other things, he helped start a local newspaper, served as a member of various boards on aging, and volunteered for Meals on Wheels. But he will long be remembered for his notorious modeling debut, in the inventive "Expose Yourself to Art" program and poster. Yup, that's Bud in the trench coat in front of the statue *Kvinneakt* on the Transit Mall (sw 5th Avenue and sw Washington Street, Downtown).

SECRET

MAZES

Imagine being plunked into a cornfield with stalks towering over 12 feet high. Everywhere you turn, it's a sea of green and gold, and just a little bit "corn-fusing." That's exactly how it is meant to be in **The MAiZE at the Pumpkin Patch on Sauvie Island** (503-621-7110, www.portlandmaze.com). Each year, a new pattern is carved into the cornfield, so you can go again and again and be even more corn-fused than before.

SECRET

MEXICAN

When the word "taco" comes to mind, I think neither fish nor vegetarian. But that doesn't stop **Taco Del Mar** (nine locations in

Portland, www.tacodelmar.com) from thinking along those lines. Fish tacos and fish burritos, along with some vegetarian dishes, are the highlights.

Good and sloppy Mexican fare with an enchilada sauce that will burn into your memory makes **Santa Fe** (831 NW 23rd Avenue, Northwest, 503-220-0406, www.santafetaqueria.com) one of the most popular Mexican eateries in Portland. Its location on "trendy-third avenue" doesn't hurt, either. In warm weather, you can sit outside and watch the people parade go by while sipping a fresh lemonade.

Chez Jose (2200 NE Broadway, Sullivan's Gulch, 503-280-9888, www.chezjoserestaurant.com) is the place to bring children. Why? Because every evening from 5 PM to 7 PM, younger children eat free! (No, your 27-year-old son does not count.) As soon as you're seated, the requisite chips and salsa appear. However, this salsa is unique to Chez Jose — mild and delicious. Try the squash enchiladas; you'll be craving them long after they are finished.

The **Ma'Tona's Restaurant** (5919 SE Foster Road, Creston-Kenilworth, 503-775-7501) is a family-run operation that serves up traditional fare in abundance. The dishes have familiar names, such as enchiladas and tacos, but the chef seems to make them rise above the mundane. Plantains, tropical fruits, and cassava are just a few of the uncommon ingredients you may find in your dish. Make sure to try the spicy-cabbage side dish. Yum!

Esparza's Tex-Mex Café (2725 SE Ankeny Street, Laurelhurst, 503-234-7909) serves up some of the best huevos rancheros in town, but all the dishes are good, homey, and filling. If you feel daring, try the Texas Ranger pork loins stuffed with napolitos (cactus). Exotic meats — ostrich, boar, buffalo, and even calf brains — make an occasional appearance on the menu. You can wash it all down with a big, potent margarita.

Esparza's is popular, so if you want to avoid a long wait, come for lunch or for an early or late dinner.

And then there's **Cinco de Mayo** (see "Secret Festivals"). Portland hosts the second-largest Cinco de Mayo celebration in the United States, largely due to its sister-city relationship with Guadalajara.

SECRET

MIDDLE EASTERN
⚜

Ya Hala (8005 SE Stark Street, Montavilla, 503-256-4484, www .yahalarestaurant.com) is the main exception to Portland's rather run-of-the-mill Middle Eastern restaurants. Yes, you'll find hummus and baba ghanouj on the menu, but this eatery elevates these staples from pedestrian to unforgettable. Even the tabbouleh is fresh and sweet. The interior is unpretentious and comfortable, with blue drapes and tiled arches. If you want to sample dishes beyond the ordinary fare, such as a kousa stew (tomatoes, zucchini, and baby squash) or sambousik (a cross between a calzone and a samosa), this is where to begin your education.

Abou Karim (221 SW Pine Street, Downtown, 503-223-5058) is a tasteful little place tucked away in an old building. If you have both carnivores and vegetarians to feed, take them here. The fare is somewhat standard, but delicious. This place is also quite kid friendly.

You wouldn't expect to find a Lebanese restaurant inside the old Bishop's House, but step inside **Al-Amir** (223 SW Stark Street, Downtown, 503-274-0010, www.alamirportland.com) and you'll be transported to the Middle East. Try the creamy hummus, smoky baba

ghanouj, and lamb dishes vibrant with spices. After a few glasses of
Lebanese beer, even the stained glass windows glow more brightly.

SECRET

MOVIES

Portlanders love their movies almost as much as they love their beer.
And where else would you expect to find a marriage of the two? The
McMenamin brothers (www.mcmenamins.com) have merged their
pubs with movie theaters at four locations. The **Bagdad Theater**
(3702 SE Hawthorne Boulevard, Sunnyside, 503-236-9234) fits perfectly into the eclectic Hawthorne neighborhood. This renovated
movie emporium bespeaks the bygone days of double features and
palatial themes. **The Mission** (1624 NW Glisan Street, Northwest,
503-223-4527) was the chain's original brewpub/theater location.
The Kennedy School (5736 NE 33rd Avenue, Concordia, 503-249-
3983) is exactly what it sounds like: a renovated elementary school.
The restaurant comes complete with cafeteria trays. No food fights,
please. And finally there is the **Edgefield Resort**, the most elegant
of the quartet (2126 SW Halsey Street, Troutdale, Oregon, 800-669-
8610). It's a great place to combine a movie with a B&B weekend.

Perhaps Portland's best single-screen movie theater is **Cinema 21**
(616 NW 21st Avenue, Northwest, 503-223-4515, www.cinema21.
com). This repertory house has a balcony, a crying room (for ba-
bies, not for sentimental movie lovers), rocking chair seats, and air
conditioning that really works. You won't find first-run flicks here.
This house specializes in movies a bit stage left — documentaries,

recent art-house releases, outrageously bad B movies, and, sometimes, a première.

Cinemagic (2021 SE Hawthorne Boulevard, Buckman, 503-231-7919) runs a movie theater the way I would. I would show what I liked, damn the crowd preference. You never know what you'll find on the marquee — *Lawrence of Arabia* or *But, I'm a Cheerleader*. A jukebox in the lobby features soundtracks from movies. And your nose does not deceive you — that is real butter on the popcorn.

The **Northwest Film Center and the Portland Art Museum** (1219 SW Park Avenue, Downtown, 503-226-2811) screens the work of the Northwest Film Center's School of Film. These two venues also host retro films and the annual Northwest Film and Video Festival, which has run for more than 25 years (www.nwfilm.org).

A movie theater coming on strong as a revival house is the **Hollywood Theatre** (4122 NE Sandy Boulevard, Hollywood, 503-281-4215). In 1926, it opened as a vaudeville theater. After its heyday with première and first-run films through the '60s, it was chopped up into three screens showing abbreviated versions of major movies. Now it's being revived with a combination of films you don't see elsewhere in the city — documentaries, classic films, experimental works, and concerts.

The **Living Room Theaters** (341 SW 10th Avenue, The Pearl, 971-222-2010, www.livingroomtheaters.com) are the next best thing to watching a flick at home. Curl up in an easy chair, couch, or occasional chair, order in your favorite beverage, and a snack or meal, and watch an independent or foreign movie in true comfort.

This city is an almost ongoing film festival with screen fests happening almost every month! In April the **Faux Film Festival** (www.fauxfilm.com) features phony movie trailers, mockumentaries, and celluloid spoofs, usually held as close as possible to April Fool's Day. May is the time for the **Portland Documentary and Experimental Film Festival** (www.pdx.filmfest.com), a jam-packed, five-day run that focuses on documentary work. The **Platform International Animation Festival** (www.platformfestival.com) hits town in June and July, with work that spans feature animation to video games and the Internet. October is the time for the **Portland Lesbian and Gay Film Festival** (www.plgff.org) with entries that range from the political to comedic. Just in time for Halloween is the **HP Lovecraft Film Festival** (www.hplfilmfestival.com) where sci-fi meets gothic horror. You could end up with squared eyeballs from watching all these movies!

Do you find that Portland seems just a bit familiar? It's no surprise. The city has had its share of Hollywood moments. Among some of the better-known films shot in Portland are *Mr. Holland's Opus*, *Body of Evidence*, and *Drugstore Cowboy*.

SECRET

MUSEUMS

The **Portland Art Museum** (1219 sw Park Avenue, Downtown, 503-226-2811) is the oldest art museum in the Pacific Northwest, and its collection spans 35 centuries. The museum attracts most of the major touring exhibitions, but its own permanent collection — which includes Native American art, Chinese artifacts, and modern European and American paintings and sculptures — is quite impressive. Every Wednesday night from April to October, the museum stops behaving like a museum and warms up with two hours of live music in the north wing.

The **Portland Children's Museum** (4105 sw Canyon Road, Washington Park, 503-223-6500, www.portlandcm.org) is the best excuse I can think of to borrow a child (if you don't have one of your own) and be young again for an afternoon. Experiment with pumps and drawbridges, play in a pint-sized diner or grocery store, and create a take-home treasure in the Clayshop. This museum is all about hands-on fun.

At the **Oregon Maritime Center and Museum** (115 sw Ash Street, Downtown, 503-224-7724), you can step back in time to an era when the local citizens used to hail passing steamboats along the Columbia and Willamette rivers. Models, photos, and navigational instruments are all part of the fascinating collection, but the sternwheeler *Steamer Portland* is the star of the show. It's even a movie star. This ship was used as a location for the filming of *Maverick* with Jodie Foster and Mel Gibson.

"Dedicated to heroes" is the theme of the **State of Oregon Sports Hall of Fame** (503-227-7466, www.oregonsportshall.org). This is the only museum of its kind in the Northwest. Feel what it's like to catch a Major League fastball in one of many interactive exhibits. And don't miss the *Put Me In, Coach* and *Over the Top* displays. Does Oregon have any sports heroes? You bet it does. The number one son appears to be Terry Baker, whose Heisman Trophy and Wall of Fame are major attractions at the museum.

If you really want to suck up some historical facts, then you definitely won't want to miss **Stark's Vacuum Cleaner Museum** (107 NE Grand Avenue, Kerns, 503-230-4101), which houses the most complete collection of vacuum cleaners in North America.

It had to happen. Someone has actually collected many, if not all, of

the black velvet paintings in the known universe and brought them together at the **Velveteria** (2448 E Burnside Street, Kerns, 503-233-5100, www.velveteria.com). What began as owners Caren Anderson and Carl Baldwin's personal holdings has evolved into a massive collection of fuzzy fine art. The collection features what you would expect: Elvis, Jesus, and lots and lots of clowns as well as some fairly unusual pieces such as the Unicorn with a comb-over.

SECRET
MUSIC
❖

Pink Martini (www.pinkmartini.com) is perhaps Portland's hottest musical exponent of international chic. As the name implies, it delivers a vibrant, stylish good time to its audiences. This 10-piece band tours nationally and abroad, while also managing to play many sold-out concerts in Portland each year. It's still enjoying the success of its first album, *Sympathetique.*

Much of the group's success and appeal can be attributed to the talents of artistic director and pianist Thomas Lauderdale. Vocalist China Forbes lends her strong and lovely voice to the music, frequently singing in French or Spanish. The result is a frothy mix of percussion, strings, and brass. One minute they're playing a bossa nova number, the next a French dance hall song. Check out their Web site for upcoming concerts.

SECRET

NEIGHBORHOODS

Old Town and **Chinatown** are so closely intertwined it's hard to tell where one stops and the other begins. Old Town Chinatown has a mysterious past. Tunnels below the streets are reminders of the days when unsavory characters shanghaied unsuspecting citizens, sailors, and loggers onto ships waiting along the riverside (see "Secret Shanghaiing"). Today, the only thing in danger may be your wallet, from all the new art and entertainment venues. Architecturally, Old Town Chinatown is worth a walk. It is reputed to have one of the largest collections of cast-iron buildings in the United States, second only to New York's SoHo district.

Chinatown makes up a significant part of Old Town Chinatown and is home to the city's traditional Chinese festivals. Kaohsiung and the People's Republic of China gave Portland an elaborate ceremonial gate (at Northwest Avenue and Burnside Street) to mark the entrance to Chinatown. You'll find the usual red brick facades and ornate lamp posts along the streets. The gem of this district is the **Portland Classical Chinese Garden** (NW 3rd Avenue and Everett Street, 503-228-8131, see "Secret Gardens").

The **Sunnyside** neighborhood, which includes part of what locals call the **Hawthorne District** (see "Secret Boho"), offers a different take on Portland life. It's the city's alternative niche, with bookstores, cafés, and quirky theaters.

The **Sellwood-Moreland** neighborhood (see "Secret Antiques") to the south is a thriving section of the city that hasn't lost touch with its village roots. And it's ready to sell you a good portion of them,

with all the antiques shops that line the streets.

Multnomah, just a short drive south of downtown, is filled with antiques shops, bookstores, and cafés. The winding, cozy streets lend it a low-key vibe.

The areas of **Alameda** and **Beaumont-Wilshire** (NE Fremont Street between 41st and 51st avenues) comprise another region where locals like to shop, eat, and browse.

S E C R E T

NIGHT OWL

Very few places in Portland, with the exception of a few convenience stores, are open 24 hours a day. But night owls should not be dismayed; there's more than a handful of late-night spots. In The Pearl, for instance, **Touché** (1425 NW Glisan Street, 503-221-1150, www.touchepdx.com) serves up pasta, pizza, and pool until 4 AM.

In boho Hawthorne, the **Montage** (301 SE Morrison Street, Buckman, 503-234-1324, www.montageportland.com) is a Creole nightspot (after all those spices, you will be awake) that serves up everything from a snack to a full meal.

Need to feel like a creature of the night? **XV** (15 SW 2nd Avenue, Downtown, 503-790-9090, www.xvpdx.com), also in Old Town Chinatown, is the dungeon in which to sport your best black and shades. The Dracula-like darkness sets the mood for late-night remedies and munchies.

A word about Old Town Chinatown: at night it can be a bit unsavory, so be streetwise and take a taxi to destinations in that area.

The turn-of-the-century environment at **Cassidy's** (1331 sw Washington Street, Downtown, 503-223-0054, www.cassidysrestaurant.com) inspires many a heavy thought and heavy conversation, but isn't that part of what night owls do — flock together and solve all the problems of the world, preferably over a good glass of wine and a veggie burger, or a belt of single-malt Scotch?

Sometimes you just have a yen, or a deep need, to grocery shop in the middle of the night. At **Zupan's Markets** (2340 w Burnside Street, Hillside, 503-497-1088, www.zupans.com), you can buy almost anything from toilet paper to fresh water chestnuts. The market is open 24 hours a day, every day, except Christmas. Nothing is bargain priced, but the market does have a deli, meat counter, and wine section.

S E C R E T

NON-SMOKING

The city of Portland has yet to decree that all restaurants should be non-smoking environments. If clean air is your number one priority when going out to dine, the following list should be of some help.

Northwest Portland: **Bluehour** (250 nw 13th Avenue, The Pearl, 503-226-3394); **BridgePort Brewpub** (1318 nw Northrup Street, The Pearl, 503-241-7179); **Harvey's Comedy Club** (436 nw 6th Avenue, Old Town Chinatown, 503-241-0338); **¡Oba!** (555 nw 12th Avenue, The Pearl, 503-228-6161); **Old Town Pizza** (226B nw Davis Street, Northwest, 503-222-9999); **Southpark Seafood Grill & Wine Bar**

(901 sw Salmon Street, The Pearl, 503-326-1300); **Wildwood** (1221 NW 21st Avenue, Northwest, 503-248-9663).

North/Northeast Portland: **Alameda Brewing Company** (4765 NE Fremont Street, Beaumont-Wilshire, 503-460-9025); **Alberta Street Public House** (1036 NE Alberta Street, King, 503-284-7665); **Laurelhurst Theater and Pub** (2735 E Burnside Street, Laurelhurst, 503-232-5511); **Laurelwood Public House & Brewery** (5115 NE Sandy Boulevard, Hollywood, 503-282-0622); **Mint** (816 N Russell Street, Eliot, 503-284-5518); **Salty's on the Columbia** (3839 NE Marine Drive, Sunderland, 503-288-4444).

Southeast Portland: **Iron Horse Restaurant** (6034 SE Milwaukie Avenue, Sellwood-Moreland, 503-232-1826); **Lucky Labrador Brewing Company** (915 SE Hawthorne Boulevard, Buckman, 503-236-3555; see "Secret Brews"); **Produce Row Café** (204 SE Oak Street, Buckman, 503-232-8355); **Skybox Pub and Grill** (sports bar; 7995 SE Milwaukie Avenue, Sellwood-Moreland, 503-731-6399).

Southwest: **Higgins** (1239 sw Broadway, Downtown, 503-222-9070); **Kells** (112 sw 2nd Avenue, Downtown, 503-227-4057; see "Secret Irish"); **Lucky Labrador Public House** (7675 sw Capitol Highway, Multnomah, 503-244-2537; see "Secret Brews"); **Porto Terra Tuscan Grill & Bar** (830 sw 6th Avenue, Downtown, 503-944-1090); **Aquaria** (470 sw Hamilton Court, Bridlemile, 503-802-5850); **Salvador Molly's** (1523 sw Sunset Boulevard, Hillsdale, 503-293-1790); **Wilf's Restaurant and Piano Bar** (800 NW 6th Avenue, inside Union Station, Downtown, 503-223-0070).

Multiple locations: **McMenamins** (www.mcmenamins.com).

SECRET

NUDITY

Public nudity is not — I repeat, not — illegal. You read me correctly. It is not against the law to take off your clothing, but please don't take this section as license to strut your stuff in the buff down Burnside Street. And while technically every beach in Oregon could be considered "clothing optional," there are two popular ones where you won't have to risk public opinion.

Sauvie Island (Route 30, west of Portland) offers **Collins Beach**, with plenty of sun and sand, and only a few perverts gazing from the safety of their boats. After you cross the bridge onto the island, stop at the first store on the left and purchase the required one-day parking pass, then head out Gillihan Road to Reeder Road. Take a right, and that will lead you to Collins Beach. Two clothing-required areas bracket the 1.15-mile nudist beach. So you'll need to wind your way through the bathing suits to the area where you can join the thongless throng.

At the far end of **Rooster Rock State Park** (I-84 east to exit 25, 503-695-2261 or 800-551-6949) is Rooster Rock, also known in the tacky vernacular as Cock Rock. This clothing-optional beach, purported to be the first sanctioned by a state park, is a little harder to find than the one on Sauvie Island. However, the rewards of the views, particularly while *au naturel*, make it well worth the walk.

SECRET

ORCHARDS

Just to the east of Portland lies a magical land filled with fruit orchards. Dozens of apple varieties, cherries, pears, blueberries, nectarines, plums, and apricots can be yours for the picking — or buying if you're not feeling up to the "u-pick" scenario. The **"Fruit Loop"** that is found along Highway 35 and Dee Highway 281 has farms and orchards that are open from April to October, depending upon what ripens and when. The "Fruit Loop" is a perfect weekend adventure, just don't blame me when you have cherry juice stains all over your favorite shirt.

SECRET

ORCHESTRAS

The oldest symphony orchestra west of St. Louis is the **Oregon Symphony** (503-228-1353, www.orsymphony.org), which calls the beautiful, if not acoustically brilliant, **Arlene Schnitzer Concert Hall** (1037 sw Broadway, Downtown, 503-248-4335) home. The orchestra has made a name for itself with colorful renditions of the large orchestral masterpieces of Rachmaninoff, Strauss, and Respighi. During its regular season, the orchestra has played host to an array of stellar visiting artists, such as Yo-Yo Ma, James Galway, and even Ray Charles, Bobby McFerrin, and Pink Martini (see "Secret Theaters").

Any city worth its salt has a major orchestra. A city with a cultural heart will also support community ensembles. The **Hillsboro Symphony Orchestra** (Hillsboro High School Auditorium, 3285 Rood Bridge Road, Hillsboro, Oregon, www.hillsborosymphony.org) is the newest addition to the local symphonic scene. The orchestra performs at least three times a year, with an emphasis on operatic tunes.

The city is also well known for its **Portland Youth Philharmonic** (421 sw 6th Avenue, Suite 1350, 503-223-5939). Dating back to 1924, the orchestra is composed of exceptional music students between the ages of 10 and 23. This outstanding ensemble is the oldest youth orchestra in the United States. You can catch a performance between November and May each year at the Arlene Schnitzer Concert Hall.

Who was Arlene Schnitzer? Back in the 1950s, she opened Portland's first major art gallery. She called it the Fountain Gallery, after the historic Skidmore Fountain only a block away. From that beginning, she went on to become a leader in the arts. Through the years, she championed many young artists. Some of the leading artists in the Northwest owe part of their success to her support and encouragement. It was really no surprise that Portland chose to honor this vibrant woman by renaming the Paramount Theater the Arlene Schnitzer Concert Hall.

SECRET

ORCHIDS

Portland Classical Chinese Garden (NW 3rd Avenue and Everett Street, Old Town Chinatown, 503-228-8131, www.portlandchinese

garden.org) is also known as the Garden of Awakening Orchids. This classical Suzhou-style garden was transported bit by bit from China and assembled by Chinese artisans. The oasis encompasses an entire city block. Within, you'll discover waterways, exotic trees, bridges, and, of course, orchids (see "Secret Gardens").

SECRET

OUTLETS

Yearn to shop at discount prices? Portland is, quietly, the place. **Columbia Sportswear**, **Nike**, **Pendleton**, and **Current** all manufacture and sell their goodies within the city, some at deeply discounted prices. Unfortunately, Jantzen has discontinued its downtown outlet.

At the **Pendleton Woolen Mills Stores** (8550 SE McLoughlin Boulevard, Milwaukie, Oregon, 503-535-5786), you'll find many prototypes for new products, and seconds of the more familiar Pendleton line. You'll find everything you need to make you a "Pendleton Woman," such as plaid skirts, wool blazers, and slacks. There's even an annex that sells buttons and zippers at deeply discounted prices.

There's no better place to find what you need to keep warm, especially on one of Portland's mid-winter drizzly days, than at the **Columbia Sportswear Outlet** (1323 SE Tacoma Street, Sellwood-Moreland, 503-238-0118). Irregulars, closeouts, and overstocks of this high-quality active gear come here fresh from the factory at up to 50 percent below retail. Just thinking about that kind of bargain makes me feel warm.

SECRET

PARKS

Portland's more than 700 parks provide plenty of space for nearly any outdoor activity in nearly every neighborhood. The Metro Greenspaces program was created in 1989 to establish and preserve a carefully linked system of natural areas throughout the city. The plan is similar to Boston's "Emerald Necklace," created by Frederick Law Olmsted in the late 19th century. The Greenspaces plan allows wildlife and hikers to travel without interruption over a nearly 40-mile loop — so be cautious when someone in Portland asks you if you'd like to go for a hike.

I've told you about lots of these places in other sections. But Portland is particularly proud of two of its parks — Forest Park (see "Secret Forests"), with its 5,000 acres of treed grounds, and Mill Ends Park.

At 24 inches square, **Mill Ends Park** (Downtown) is the world's smallest dedicated park. You'll find it in the median strip at the corner of SW Naito Parkway and Taylor Street. Its story began when a journalist for the *Oregonian*, Dick Fagan, got tired of seeing an ugly pothole below his window. He decided to plant some flowers in the hole and name it Mill Ends Park. To generate some interest in this miniscule green space, Fagan centered many newspaper stories on the capers of a fictitious park resident, a leprechaun named Patrick O'Toole. Rumor has it that the park has been the site of several weddings, but no wedding permit has ever been issued by the parks department. The park is open year-round and there's no admission fee.

S E C R E T

PDX

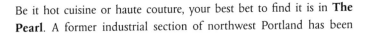

As airports go, Portland appears still spanking new and sparkling after some major renovations over the past few years. You will find vast areas currently underutilized given Delta's retreat from Portland as a hub for flights to Asia, but for the most part the airport is a user-friendly facility. The shopping mall that connects the terminals hosts a good selection of shops selling Oregon-oriented wares and even two outlets of **Powell's Books**. Notably, Powell's has the courage to sell used books in an airport. This tactic may not generate the funds necessary to maintain a pricey location, but it certainly endears the store to about-to-depart bibliophiles.

Made In Oregon (PDX Terminal, 503-282-7827 or 503-335-6563) features some of the best Oregon crafts, wines, and comestibles (okay, jellies and jams). The airport location is perfect for last-minute, oh-my-gawd-I-forgot-a-gift-for-the-pet-sitter buying sprees.

A new MAX light-rail line links the airport to the downtown core and to points east and west of the city. You board the train inside the airport, only a short distance from the baggage area.

S E C R E T

PEARL

Be it hot cuisine or haute couture, your best bet to find it is in **The Pearl**. A former industrial section of northwest Portland has been turned into a thriving community of arts and commerce. The Pearl is home to galleries, brewmeisters, chefs, artists, and designers. The brick-and-steel landscape left behind by heavy industry has been transformed into trendy retail spaces, eclectic galleries, and upscale lofts.

Why "The Pearl"? The name originated in the 1980s from the observation that galleries and lofts secreted in post-industrial buildings were like pearls hidden in oysters.

The **Portland Institute for Contemporary Art** (224 NW 13th Avenue, 503-242-1419, www.pica.org) has recently made its home in a remodeled warehouse, adding to The Pearl's important art scene. New boutiques, restaurants, and cafés appear to open almost every month, so don't expect your favorite patisserie or bistro to experience a long life. **Powell's** bookstore (1005 W Burnside Street, 503-228-4651) anchors the district, but you will find more than print to lure you here. Goodies within the Pearl include European-style linens at the **French Quarter** (1313 NW Glisan Street, 503-282-8200, www.frenchquarterlinens.com); provincial antiques at **Thea's Interiors** (1204 NW Glisan Street, 503-274-0275, www.theasinteriors.com); rare and unusual jewelry at **Judith Arnell** (320 NW 10th Avenue, 503-227-3437, www.juditharnell.com); and handmade floral papers at **Oblation Papers and Press** (516 NW 12th Avenue, 503-223-1093, www.oblationpapers.com).

Tucked among all the upscale galleries and antique shops is the **Dehen Knitting Company's Factory Outlet Store** (1040 NW 44th Street, Northeast, 503-222-3871), a haven for those of you who may have lost your letterman sweater or are in desperate need of a cheerleader's outfit. The sweats are high quality, as are the sweaters, and it's not essential to add pompoms to your shopping cart.

If you are lucky enough to be in Portland over the Labor Day weekend, you'll have a chance to experience **Art in The Pearl** (503-

722-9017, www.artinthepearl.com), an annual arts and crafts festival. What's the ideal way to view The Pearl? By streetcar. The new Portland Streetcar links The Pearl with the Northwest neighborhood and Downtown (see "Secret Streetcars").

S E C R E T

PENNY

It all began in 1843, when Tennessee drifter William Overton and Massachusetts lawyer Asa Lovejoy beached their canoe on the banks of the Willamette River. Overton immediately saw the potential in this mountain-ringed, timber-rich land. His only problem was that he lacked the 25 cents required to file a land claim. So he struck a bargain with Lovejoy: in return for a quarter, Overton would share his claim to the 640 acres known as "The Clearing."

Soon bored with clearing trees and building roads, Overton drifted on, selling his half of the claim to Francis W. Pettygrove. The new partners, Lovejoy and Pettygrove, had difficulty settling on a name for their budding township. Lovejoy was determined that it should be named for his hometown of Boston, while Pettygrove was equally adamant about his native Portland. They decided to flip a coin, now known as the "Portland Penny," to settle the argument. Pettygrove won on two tosses out of three. So where's the penny? Where else but the **Oregon History Center** (1200 sw Park Avenue, Downtown, 503-222-1741, see "Secret History")?

SECRET

PERIODICALS

Portland's sole daily newspaper is the **Oregonian**, now with only a morning edition. The Friday paper contains a weekly arts and entertainment section called, appropriately, A&E. There's also the twice-weekly **Portland Tribune**, which focuses more on the "inside scoops" of the city. **Willamette Week** is the city's alternative newspaper. The principal gay and lesbian tabloid is a monthly called **Just Out**.

With the exception of the *Portland Tribune*, most of the "little" papers are free. Portland is a big, big book town, and that includes print of all kinds. You'll find distribution boxes all over the city for *Willamette Week* and *Just Out*. As well, many neighborhoods produce their own gazette-type papers.

SECRET

PERSONALITY

After you've been here a few days, you'll begin to notice it. A particular vibe. A certain stubbornness. A kind of "I'll do it my way, dammit" philosophy. Yup, you have just discovered the Portland personality. This yen to keep dancing to a different drummer gives Portland its own unique style.

While Seattle was busy tearing up its old downtown and making way for new freeways and skyscrapers, Portland preserved its architectural heritage. Instead of simply adding more office space, Portland added sculptures and fountains to its downtown core. And while Seattle spends big bucks for sports teams and the facilities they require, Portland remains content with its Trail Blazers and a very efficient light-rail system.

So beneath the ponytails, beards, Levi's, and tie-dye, you'll find very independent souls who actually think about their neighbors and neighborhoods more often than they think about themselves.

SECRET

PHOTO OPS

Driving around the city, you'll be astounded at how frequently Mount Hood will be visible from your window. On clear days, you'll be tempted to pull over and just drink in the incredible beauty of this peak. Movie producers were quick to see its photogenic qualities: Mount Hood was used in the movie musical *Lost Horizon*.

How many photos of Portland have you seen with the snow-covered cap of Mount Hood looming in the background? If you want to snap a similar photo while you're visiting, there are a number of good places to try. Most popular are the terraces of the **International Rose Test Garden** and the pavilion at the **Japanese Garden** (for both, see "Secret Gardens"). You can get another great view from the grounds of the **Pittock Mansion** (see "Secret Mansion").

You can enjoy one of the city's best views from atop a butte in a ridgetop neighborhood in West Hills. At 1,073 feet above sea level, this is the highest point within the city limits. Council Crest is home to such celebrities as filmmaker Gus Van Sant. From the summit, the panorama of the Tualatin Valley and Washington County to the west is worth a look, particularly at sunset. On the eastern side, steps lead up to an observation platform with arrows indicating five Cascades peaks. Even if the mountains are hiding behind a few clouds, the view of Downtown and the rest of the city will take your breath away.

SECRET

PIANO BARS

A piano bar in an Amtrak station? Yes, indeed. **Wilf's Restaurant and Piano Bar** (800 NW 6th Avenue, Downtown, 503-223-0070, www.wilfsrestaurant.com), an old-fashioned nightclub inside Union Station, features pianists playing Sinatra-like standards. Sip a cosmopolitan in its own beaker of crushed ice and pretend you're the vixen in a film noir feature from the 1940s. You almost expect Archie Goodwin, of "Nero Wolfe" fame, to walk through the door at any moment, a fedora slouched over one eye.

The dueling pianos are straight from *The Fabulous Baker Boys*, but the real attraction may be the navel-baring waitresses at **Boogie Woogies** (915 SW 2nd Avenue, 503-417-8717). At the request of the noisy, mostly middle-aged crowd, two piano players perform the most standard of standard repertoires. John Denver, Journey, and REO Speedwagon may not be everyone's cup of tea, but the music has a strange allure. Throughout the show, everyone seems to get into the act, including the barkeeps. They sing, they dance (even on top of the beautiful wooden bar), and they seem to be having the best time ever.

Boogie Woogies also doubles as a singles bar. Every Tuesday, men and women rotate around the bar, answering questions and looking for love. If you want to participate, be sure to arrive by 6:30 PM.

S E C R E T
PIZZA

It's late. You're hungry. It's early. You're hungry. It's any time of the day, and you want a pizza! Try **Escape from New York Pizza** (622 NW 23rd Avenue, Northwest, 503-227-5423), a no-frills joint serving up pizza with red sauce, lots of cheese, and traditional toppings. Head somewhere else if you want substitutions or unusual bits atop your pizza.

Pizzicato (20 locations in the Porland area, www.pizzicatopizza .com) serves up the pesto and sun-dried tomato variety of pizza, but you can get just the basics as well. Its location on "trendy-third" doesn't hurt the establishment. Grab a slice and wander down the street under a canopy of trees festooned with little twinkling lights.

S E C R E T
POLICE

Can't get enough of handcuffs and guns? Try the **Portland Police Historical Museum** (1111 SW 2nd Avenue, 16th Floor, Downtown,

503-823-0019, www.portlandpolicemuseum.com). This kitschy excursion into the history of law enforcement is pretty entertaining. You'll see everything from a somewhat outdated display of drugs and their slang names to a collection of homemade but very efficient weapons, including those made in prison. There are also badges, uniforms, and old jail cells. The museum is on the 16th floor of the Justice Center Building, so you'll need to show some photo ID to get through the front door. And be prepared for a bit of a wait for an elevator — this is a busy place.

SECRET
PORTLAND-SPEAK

Want to sound like a local, or at least understand what some of the locals are saying? Here's a quick compendium of some local nicknames for landmarks, highways, and some institutions.

Route 26 is called the Sunset Highway, while I-84 is known as the Banfield Highway. The US Bancorp Tower is nicknamed the Big Pink. The Arlene Schnitzer Concert Hall is fondly spoken of as the Schnitz. The I-405 bridge across the Willamette River is better known as the Fremont Bridge, and the I-5 bridge across the Willamette is called the Marquam Bridge. And Portland's light-rail system is affectionately named the MAX.

SECRET

PRIDE

Portland has a gay scene but, like all things in the city, it's low key. To find out the most up-to-date information, pick up a copy of *Just Out* (www.justout.com), a free monthly publication covering news, arts, and community events. The most complete listings can be found in Portland's *Gay and Lesbian Community Yellow Pages* (www.pdxgayyellowpages.com).

The hub of Portland's gay bar nightlife is the Downtown neighborhood flanking Stark Street and sw 11th Avenue. **Embers** (110 NW Broadway, 503-222-3082, www.emberspdx.net) will make you believe that the '70s never died. The crowd is mixed — gay, lesbian, and straight — and the DJ is top notch. **Hobo's** (120 NW 3rd Avenue, 503-224-3285, www.hobospdx.com), strictly for the guys, is a piano bar housed in an historic old storefront.

The **Egyptian Club** (3701 SE Division Street, Richmond, 503-236-8689, www.eroompdx.com) is the center of the Sapphic social scene in the city. There are lots of activities — DJ dancing Thursdays to Saturdays, pool, karaoke, and other special events.

Portland's **Gay Pride Parade and Celebration** (503-295-9788, www.pridenw.org) usually takes place in late June and attracts some 10,000 participants.

S E C R E T

QUINTESSENCE

The very quintessence of Portland's culinary flavor was once found at the tiny and informal Caprial and Caprial's Bistro. They are now closed, but have since been reinvented as **Caprial and John's Kitchen** (609 SE Ankeny Street, Downtown, 503-239-8771, www .caprialandjohnskitchen.com), a working kitchen with a communal table to share the night's menu. The "Supper Club" is by reservation only, and features a prix fixe ever-changing menu.

For seafood, there's **Jake's Famous Crawfish** (401 SW 12th Avenue, Downtown, 503-226-1419), which captures more of the city's charm than many other, fussier establishments. Fresh seafood and a vibrant bar scene make this vintage landmark perpetually popular.

And don't forget the McMenamin brothers' restaurant/bar/theaters (see "Secret Brothers"). They truly do represent the quintessence of Portland's creative decades.

S E C R E T

RAILS

The **Oregon Zoo Railway** (4001 SW Canyon Road, Washington Park, 503-226-1561, www.oregonzoo.org) is the only surviving railroad post office, so be sure to mail a postcard while you're aboard. The train runs between the zoo and the Rose Garden. Along with the scenery, you'll get a little Oregon history.

The restored cars of the **Mount Hood Railroad** (110 Railroad Avenue, Hood River, Oregon, 800-872-4661, www.mthoodrr.com) chug from Hood River to Parkdale, March to December, linking the Columbia Gorge to Mount Hood. The rail service has operated since 1906, when it served as an economic lifeline for the Hood River Valley. In the 1920s and '30s, the railroad was also a commuter train. Today, the operation is strictly for tourists and offers a rare view of the Hood River Valley, with Mount Hood and Mount Adams supplying a dramatic backdrop. You can take a simple excursion, or ride the dinner or brunch trains.

You can even find rails in miniature. The **Molalla Miniature Train** (31803 s Shady Dell Road, Molalla, Oregon, 503-829-6866, www .pnls.org) is southeast of downtown Portland. Hobbyist volunteers drive this miniature steam train along a 0.7-mile route. Passengers can bring their lunch and relax in a shaded picnic area, before or after riding the finely detailed train.

And, finally, there is **Amtrak** and **Union Station** (800 NW 6th Avenue, Downtown). The station is a throwback to the glamorous era of rail travel, with its prominent clock tower, great curving entrance, and muscular features. The station opened on Valentine's Day of 1896 and is the nation's oldest continuously operating train depot. The wonderful clocks atop the tower have been wound by hand daily since the station opened. Trains arrive and leave daily for points east, south, and north. So heed the retro neon sign that urges you to "take the train" for a leisurely sojourn.

S E C R E T

RELAY
❁

Okay, you and 11 friends decide you'd like to spend the weekend at the beach, but you have no car. No problem. Just join the **Hood to Coast Relay** (503-292-4626, www.hoodtocoast.com). After all, it's only 195 miles to the ocean. Tiring as it may sound, the August relay has long been an annual event. Registration is limited to 1,000 teams of 8 to 12 people, and participants raise money for the American Cancer Society. The 2009 run raised over $360,000 for charity. Though it's technically a race, participants enter the HTC for its traveling circus tendencies. In 2002, for example, the "Twelve Elvises" ran dressed as the King.

The madness begins at the Timberline Lodge, 6,000 feet up Mount Hood. The course winds through the heart of Portland and into the thick forests of western Oregon, finally emerging at the sea. If you are in downtown Portland on the day of the event, head for the **Old Spaghetti Factory** (715 SW Bancroft Street, Homestead, 503-222-5375). There's lots of parking, and plenty of space to watch the race go by.

S E C R E T

RIVER
❁

There are two misconceptions about Portland. The first is that it is a port city on the ocean, like Portland, Maine. Not true. The second is that the Columbia River dominates the city. Also not true. While the Columbia *is* very important to the city and provides deep-water access to the ocean, another river defines the city. Portland grew up on both banks of the Willamette River, where it flows into the Columbia. Fourteen of Portland's bridges span the Willamette; only two interstate bridges cross the Columbia. And here's a bit of river trivia — the Willamette is the longest north-flowing river in the continental United States.

Want to sound like a local? As any local will tell you, "It's will-AM-mit, dammit."

S E C R E T

ROMANCE

A table for two. Isn't that what romance is all about? You couldn't find a better table for two than at **Lucy's Table** (704 NW 21st Avenue, Northwest, 503-226-6126, www.lucystable.com), a sumptuous yet funky spot with provocative art on the walls. The wait staff knows how to pamper you and the exotic menu will have you thinking you've arrived at a Robin Leach hangout. The menu includes such delicacies as pomegranate-basted ribs, charred squid, and cold almond and garlic soup. And the desserts. Ah, the desserts. Flourless chocolate cake, crème brûlée, and homemade ice creams. You might almost forget why you came here to set a romantic scene. A nice surprise is the wide-ranging and affordable wine list.

The London Grill (Benson Hotel, 309 SW Broadway, Downtown, 503-295-4110) is romantic with an upscale twist. This Portland institution has been serving up both fine dinners and lush scenery for decades. The opulent chandeliers and overstuffed seats are just a prelude to the menu. Chateaubriand for two, chicken Oscar, and veal medallions speak of the restaurant's heritage, while such up-tempo items as ahi fillet and ostrich show this establishment knows how to keep up with the times.

Want to take a magic carpet ride with your romance? Step inside the **Marrakesh** (1201 NW 21st Avenue, Northwest, 503-248-9442, www.marrakeshportland.com) and you'll find yourself in a scene straight out of *A Thousand and One Nights*. Soft fabrics drape the walls and form tent-like structures, while low lights and low tables complete the atmosphere. Since you won't be eating with a fork, dinner plays like a scene from *Tom Jones*, if it had been set in Morocco. The food isn't quite up to fabulous, but the atmosphere is, so go and feast on the ambiance.

Bluehour (250 NW 13th Avenue, The Pearl, 503-226-3394, www.blue houronline.com) raised the bar for romance, and dining in general, in the city. Every detail of this chic restaurant begs to be noticed: the panels of shimmering fabric draped to the black walnut floors, a fleet of butter-soft leather chairs. Don't think this restaurant is all show, however. The menu deserves equal attention, with its offerings of Mediterranean classics such as insalata caprese, and potato gnocchi brought uptown with a fontina and truffle sauce.

Where better to savor a romantic evening than at **Iorio** (912 SE Hawthorne Boulevard, Sunnyside, 503-445-4716, www.ioriorestaurant .com). This Italian favorite has a fireplace and a very comfortable atmosphere that puts you in the mood for some fantastic Italian cuisine, among other things.

A cozy setting, a glass of wine, and thou. Well, it's not quite a poem from the *Rubiyat* but **Wine Down** (126 NE 28th Avenue, Kerns, 503-236-9463, www.winedownpdx.com) will certainly put you in a poetic mood. This dimly lit, cozy setting is the perfect place to cuddle up with someone and a special vintage. To end the evening, try something from their extensive port menu.

ROOMS WITH A VIEW

You can ask for a room with a view in this city, but that won't guarantee the weather will cooperate for a truly spectacular sunset. If you are determined, however, here are some ideas.

You can find views of a different kind at the **Hotel Vintage Plaza** (422 sw Broadway, Downtown, 503-228-1212 or 800-263-2305, www.vintageplaza.com). Cleverly angled skylights give a loft-like feel to the small, comfortable rooms. The skylights are intriguing no matter what the weather.

Hotel Fifty (50 sw Morrison Street, Downtown, 503-221-0711 or 877-237-6775, www.hotelfifty.com) located across the park from the Willamette has splendid view of the river, and a glimpse of the fabulous '50s. This hotel is so cool, daddy-o. This place is perfect for your own Kerouac-style journey. The rooms are furnished in the retro "Danish modern" and represent all that was the best of this era.

The **RiverPlace Hotel** (1510 sw Harbor Way, Downtown, 503-228-3233 or 800-227-1333, www.riverplacehotel.com) is a fairly standard, but pricey, modern hotel. The rooms are large and the décor is peppy — lots of blue to reflect its marine theme. What you pay for here is a strip of real estate with a river view.

If you don't want to stay all night, have dinner at the RiverPlace's

Three Degrees Restaurant (503-295-6166, www.threedegrees restaurant.com), where picture windows overlook the river. The river traffic might distract you from the food, but don't let that happen. The Continental menu, featuring upscale choices such as medallions of beef and rack of lamb, is as good as the view. Three Degrees is also a good place for Sunday brunch.

The Chart House (5700 sw Terwilliger Boulevard, Hillsdale, 503-246-6963, www.chart-house.com) undeniably has the best view of the Willamette and downtown Portland of any restaurant in the city. Yes, it's part of a chain, but the clam chowder is so good that it won an award in Boston! The menu is mostly seafood, but there are steaks for those in your party who refuse to eat fish. Most importantly, save room for the chocolate lava cake. You have to order this at the start of your meal or it won't be ready when you are. Mmm, mmm, good.

SECRET

ROOT BEER

Creamy. Spicy. Complex. Peppery. Although those adjectives could apply to a newly released microbrew, they also apply to a newly created root beer.

Not that long ago, root beer was the soda-pop flavor of choice. Long before there was Pepsi and Mountain Dew, there was root beer, the drink that defined an era of drive-in hamburger stands, soda fountains, and simpler times. These days, it's making a comeback in Portland's brewpubs. Why? Because the brewpubs are becoming more family oriented, like English pubs, so you need to have a beverage for the kids.

Originally, root beer was a fermented blend of yeast, sugar, and liquid of roots and barks. Sarsaparilla and sassafras were most commonly used. In 1865 a Philadelphia pharmacist, Charles E. Hires, began bottling his concoction, and it soon became a popular product. During Prohibition, breweries began bottling root beer, and many continue to do so.

So, go ahead, take your kids to a brewpub, where they can enjoy a local brew with you. You might even try one yourself, if you happen to be the designated driver. Look for home-brewed root beer at the **Laurelwood Public House & Brewery** (5115 NE Sandy Boulevard, 503-282-0622) or the **Pyramid Brewing Company** (2730 NW 31st Avenue, Northwest, 503-228-5269).

S E C R E T

ROSES

Portland is known as the Rose City, and certainly the city blooms with them in the most unexpected places. But did you know that in the **Rose Quarter** (1 N Center Court Street, Downtown, 503-235-8771, www.rosequarter.com), there are no roses? The Rose Quarter is a huge complex that includes the massive 20,000-seat Rose Garden, home to the NBA Trail Blazers; the 12,000-seat Memorial Coliseum; and the Rose Quarter Commons, with its high-intensity water-jet fountain.

You can stop to smell the roses in almost everyone's backyard. But it you don't want to be arrested for trespassing, head for the **International Rose Test Garden** (400 SW Kingston Avenue, Washington Park, 503-227-7033, www.rosegardenstore.org, see "Secret Gardens").

The garden is home to more than 550 species of roses. When they're in full bloom, you could count more than 8,000 blossoms, if you had the time.

But what about the "test" part of the garden? Are the roses judged on intelligence? Physical strength? "Rose Test" refers to the fact that the garden is one of 24 official testing sites for the All-American Rose selections; the roses are chosen by a group of commercial rose growers and hybridizers in the US. Just be sure you don't touch the roses in the garden. The fine for trying to take some home is a steep $250. Did I forget to mention that the Mme. Caroline Testout is the official city rose?

If you need to "gather ye roses while ye may," and keep them for the trip home, try the **Rose Garden Store** (850 SW Rose Garden Way, Washington Park, 503-227-7033, www.rosegardenstore.org). It stocks rose-themed merchandise, including rose-patterned tea sets, floral wreaths, and just about anything on which you could pin a rose.

SECRET

SAGA
❖

Like all good Western cities, Portland's history reads more like a good saga. So gather round. Are you sitting comfortably? Then let's begin.

Portland sits on land that originally was home to the Chinook Indians. Early in the 19th century, the Columbia River captured the attention of one Thomas Jefferson. During an expedition set forth by the President, the explorers Lewis and Clark came across the site that would become Portland. Little more than a clearing in a forest on the Willamette River, halfway between Fort Vancouver and Willamette Falls, it was largely a rest stop for fur traders and natives en route between those two places.

Ocean commerce would bring settlers to Portland in the 1840s. Ocean-going ships favored the deep port, which today is the largest inland port in the United States, 100 miles upriver from the mouth of the Columbia.

The earliest plan for the city, in 1845, called for small city blocks. Rumor has it that this was done to ensure there were numerous desirable corner lots. Whatever the reason, it was a good idea. Today, because of these short blocks, Portland is one of the most walkable cities in America.

To encourage growth on the new frontier, Congress passed an act in 1850 that provided every adult white male settler with 320 acres of land in Oregon. Unfortunately, that act conflicted directly with a 1787 law that promised the US would not take Native American lands without natives' consent. It set off a devastating series of conflicts. By 1851, half of the Willamette Valley and all of the lower Columbia was surrendered to the United States through a series of 13 treaties that guaranteed Native Americans the remainder of the land. Sadly, by 1855, the natives had all been relocated to reservations east of the Cascade Mountains.

Over time, Oregon has passed some curious laws. In 1843, with the creation of the Oregon Country, slavery was outlawed. Unfortunately, so were blacks. The first Oregon exclusion law, passed in 1844, required all blacks to leave the territory within three years.

In 1857, Oregon voters chose to make their territory a state. In the same election, they overwhelmingly opposed slavery but reaffirmed the exclusion law. This law, although largely unenforced, remained a part of the Oregon constitution until 1926.

Portland grew rapidly with the approach of the 20th century, due in no small part to the completion of the transcontinental railway. In fact, its progress was so rapid that the 1905 Lewis and Clark Centennial Exhibition drew people from across the country. The Olmsted Brothers of Massachusetts were hired to design the Centennial Exposition, but instead ended up creating a comprehensive parks system for the city, with playgrounds and waterfront parks.

Another growth spurt followed the fair. By 1913, Portland's population had doubled to almost 276,000 residents. Again, the railway was at the center of this population explosion, with the completion of the Union Pacific, North Pacific, and Great Northern lines.

For most of the 20th century, Portland has remained a stable, steady city of commerce. The advent of World War II saw a boom in the shipbuilding industry, and then Portland slipped back into a more temperate economy.

With the election of governor Tom McCall, things began to change. Portland became a leader in environmental issues — first in the cleanup of the Willamette River, and later in the innovations of its transit system. Today, the city is a model for urban planners. Most recently, Portlanders have taken up the cause of the salmon. In 1999, the salmon and steelhead that swim up the Willamette through Portland were added to the federal government's endangered species list. That act kicked off a campaign to make sure that all future development would be "salmon friendly."

So the saga continues. From seemingly ultra-conservative, almost bigoted, beginnings, a more liberal, environmentally conscious state has emerged. It will be interesting to see what happens in the future.

SECRET
SATURDAYS

As the Sandpipers once sang, "Come Saturday morning, I'm going away with my friend." And if that friend agrees, we're going straight to the **Portland Saturday Market** (108 w Burnside Street, Old Town Chinatown, 503-222-6072, www.saturdaymarket.org). The market, founded in 1974, is the largest continuously operating outdoor arts and crafts market in the us. It's filled with colors and flavors straight from the 1960s. If you've ever wondered what happened to tie-dye, your question will be answered here — it all went to Portland. Located in the heart of Old Town Chinatown, under the Burnside Bridge, the market is great fun. The credo for the items for sale is "Make it, bake it, or grow it." This doesn't mean it's all down-home hookahs and crochet. No sir. Sophisticated art is available from talented artisans. The market is open every Saturday and Sunday, rain or shine (that's why it's under the bridge), from March until Christmas Eve.

On the fringes of the market, temporary booths with more traditional flea-market fare and food emporiums flogging such delicacies as corn dogs appear, but the real Saturday market is under the bridge. Take the MAX train, as parking is unbelievably dismal.

S E C R E T

SCANDAL

If you look for the town of Vanport on a map, you won't find it. This wartime housing project, built in 1942 on a flood plain, served 18,700 shipyard workers and their families. Its construction was such a rush job that a congressional investigating committee criticized not just the buildings themselves, but also most of the area's public services. African-Americans, who lived in a segregated area of the project, and women made up a large portion of the workforce. Shifts ran 24 hours a day to keep up the wartime production needed.

After the war, many residents stayed. The day before Memorial Day in 1948, an engineer inspected the entire dike system around the project and reported that all was well. Unfortunately, part of the dike had been built around a rotting train trestle, filled simply by tossing materials over the side to bury it. Recent heavy rains and melting snow had swelled the Columbia River to record levels, and moisture seeped into the dike.

A siren went off on May 30, 1948, just as a six-foot wall of water crashed into Vanport. Many people didn't hear the signal, and because previous reports had insisted that warnings would sound well in advance, the response was slow. Some people tried to help neighbors and collect belongings before they realized, in the words of one store owner, that "life, not property, was the question." Within minutes, the break widened to 600 feet, and within two hours, up to 20 feet of debris-filled water covered the town.

Witnesses saw floating cars crushed by buildings, men in small boats breaking into upper-floor windows, and frightened residents being evacuated at gunpoint by police. Hundreds fled on foot and traffic jammed the few exit routes. Surprisingly, there were only 15 casualties, because many people were not at home when it happened, but the town was completely lost.

Almost all of the buildings were destroyed. The decision to build on such a treacherous area was questionable, but the subsequent treatment of the flood victims, 25 percent of whom were African-Americans, was scandalous. Today, you won't find any reference to Vanport on city maps. But if you visit West Delta Park, you will know what is underneath it.

SECRET

SCENTS

Want to sniff an exotic scent? **The Perfume House** (3328 SE Hawthorne Boulevard, Sunnyside, 503-234-5375, www.theperfumehouse .com) is possibly the ultimate in olfactory satisfaction. The house has been praised by the likes of Yves St. Laurent and Jean Patou as the finest in the world. You can even smell the elusive and very expensive Corina from Patrician House, which was introduced at the Seattle World's Fair in 1962 and is considered one of the greatest perfumes ever created. Myself, I still think Joy heads the list.

Escential Lotions and Oils (3638 SE Hawthorne Boulevard, Sunnyside, 800-750-6457, www.escential.net) is a terrific place to put together a gift basket for someone special, or simply to indulge yourself. This store puts bath oils and lotions into a whole new stratosphere. You can even create your own special concoction.

SECRET

SCHOOL

You'll have no fear of waking to a flying chalkboard eraser at **The Kennedy School** (5736 NE 33rd Avenue, Concordia, 503-249-3983 or 888-249-3983), where the only thing you'll be studying is counting sheep. In 1997, the McMenamin brothers turned the 84-year-old school's classrooms into guest rooms and kept all the appropriate trappings, including each room's original blackboard.

SECRET

SCIENCE

Want to know where you can touch a tornado? Feel an earthquake? Head to the waterfront and the **Oregon Museum of Science and Industry**, or OMSI (1945 SE Water Avenue, Downtown, 503-797-4000, www.omsi.edu). This is a museum that can truly say it's come a long way, baby. From its humble beginnings on the hill near the zoo, it has morphed into a spectacular facility with six immense exhibit halls, a planetarium, an IMAX theater, a naval submarine (the USS *Blueback*), and a café. Does the submarine seem familiar? It was used for part of the filming of *The Hunt for Red October*. Inside the museum, you can poke around an old turbine engine, virtually experience a tornado or an earthquake, or cruise the Internet.

The Murdock Planetarium is especially fun. Its Digistar system can simulate three-dimensional space travel. You won't have any trouble

finding this building, with its distinctive fire-engine red smokestack, glass pyramid atrium, and copper cap.

S E C R E T

SCOTLAND
✣

The **Scottish Country Shop** (1450 SE Powell Boulevard, Richmond, 503-238-2528 or 800-550-3568, www.scottishcountryshop.com) will whisk you into a wee bit of the Highlands, with its cornucopia of foods, teas, jewelry, kilts, bagpipes, tin whistles, ties, and tartans. It stocks everything you need to create a Scots atmosphere, with the exception of Mel Gibson in a kilt.

Head to the **Rose & Thistle Pub** (2314 NE Broadway, Sullivan's Gulch, 503-287-8582) for a taste of Scotland. It's the only Scottish pub in Portland — which means it leans a little heavily on grease and salt for its authentic flavor.

S E C R E T

SEEDS
✣

In the 1940s, a Chinese forester came across a remote grove of unusual trees. It turned out that the seeds of these trees were a match — holy DNA, Batman! — for the fossilized remains of the dawn redwood. The seeds were sent to the United States and planted in the **Hoyt Arboretum** (4000 SW Fairview Boulevard, Washington

Park, 503-865-8733, www.hoytarboretum.org), where they took hold. In just four years, the trees bore cones — the first dawn redwood cones produced in the western hemisphere in 50 million years. So when you go visit the Arboretum, you can ooh and ahh over the delicate silk trees, but the real awe belongs to the dawn redwoods, rare deciduous conifers.

SECRET

SHAKESPEARE

"A rose by any other name would smell as sweet," but almost nowhere else will you find an entire garden devoted to the flowers mentioned in the works of the immortal Bard. The **International Rose Test Garden** (see "Secret Gardens") devotes a worthy space to a worthy playwright.

SECRET

SHANGHAIING

What is "shanghaiing" and what does it have to do with Portland? Shanghaiing was an illegal maritime practice in which able-bodied men — sailors, loggers, vagabonds, or other hard workers — were kidnapped and sold to sea captains, who forced them to work aboard their ships for no pay. In Portland, a series of trap doors, also known as dead falls, were used to drop unsuspecting victims into the "Portland Underground" system of tunnels. From 1850 to as late as 1941, sailors called Portland the Unheavenly City or the Forbidden City due to this shocking practice. During shanghaiing's heyday, at least 1,500 people were shanghaied out of Portland every year.

It wasn't just able-bodied men who were secreted out of the city. In Portland's early days, women had to be especially cautious when venturing into certain areas. They were warned not to go to dances and to stay out of restaurants, saloons, and other establishments of the evening. They, too, became victims of this shadowy and scandalous part of the city's history. Women who were kidnapped found themselves dragged or carried through the tunnels and sold into "white slavery." These women seemed to vanish and were never heard from again.

The Portland Underground, better known as the "Shanghai Tunnels," was a series of basements connected to other buildings through brick and stone archways, intersected by tunnels. These catacombs ran all along the Portland waterfront, from the North End (today's Old Town Chinatown to Skidmore Fountain) to the South End (Downtown).

The most notorious of the shanghai bullies was hotelier Joseph "Bunco" Kelly. He often bragged that he could gather a full ship's crew in less than 12 hours. One evening, in his quest to fulfill his boast, Kelly ran across a group who had stumbled upon the open cellar of a mortuary. Thinking the cellar was part of the Snug Harbor Pub, the men had consumed cups of embalming fluid, which they had mistaken for liquor. When Kelly found them, several had died and others were dying. Claiming the dead were merely unconscious from too much drink, Kelly sold all 22 to a captain whose ship sailed before the truth was known.

In another attempt to make a quick buck, Kelly delivered a dime-store Indian heavily wrapped in blankets to a ship. When the captain learned the next morning that his new crew member was a wooden statue, he became so angry that he threw it overboard. It was recovered by two men operating a dredge nearly 60 years later.

Some of the passages still exist. The **Cascade Geographic Society** (503-622-4798, cgsmthood@onemain.com) conducts tours, by appointment only. The 90-minute tours are held in the evening, when shanghaiing usually took place. If you want to experience this creepy environment firsthand, be prepared to handle some rickety stairs, dust, dirt, musty smells, and anything else you can think of that lurks below ground. If you need a mask, make sure to bring your own. And dress appropriately — no high heels, sandals, thongs, or open-toed shoes.

SECRET

SHOPPING

Portland has oodles of shopping centers, a plethora of trendy districts filled with boutiques, and a handful of outlet stores. But everyone shops at Freddie's. **Fred Meyers** stores are an institution. They are not ordinary grocery stores. In fact, Fred Meyers may well have been the original concept in superstores. You'll find everything from groceries to gardening supplies, bed linens to electronics, hardware to children's toys. Over the years, Freddie's has grown to include in-store banks, photo processing kiosks, bakeries, and even Starbucks in the newer locations. Go on — live like a Portlander.

Pick up some deli treats for a picnic while you grab a can of oil for the car, and don't forget to check out the jewelry counter for a special souvenir of the city.

One of the nicest things about Portland is that it has kept its downtown thriving. While mall mania has struck many an American city, Portland has gone out of its way to maintain its glorious shopping core. At the top of the list of places to shop in the city is **Macy's** (621 sw 5th Avenue, Downtown, 503-223-0512), once known as Meier and Frank, a mainstay in the city since 1857. It has everything you would expect from a department store including a beauty salon, a bridal registry, and a place for ladies-who-lunch, the Georgian Room.

The staff at **Nordstrom** (701 sw Broadway, Downtown, 503-224-6666) is still as helpful as ever, and the sales are worth standing in line for. This downtown location was the first in Oregon, but the Washington Square branch (9700 sw Washington Square Road, 503-620-0555) is much bigger.

Now we head to the malls, beginning with the **Jantzen Beach SuperCenter** (1405 Jantzen Beach Center, Hayden Island, 503-286-9103, www.jantzenbeachsupercenter.com). Do not take the word "super" lightly. This is 800,000 square feet of shopping, with 20 major retailers and 45 specialty stores. Best of all, it's tax-free! You'll find everything in one place: Linens 'n' Things, Old Navy, Circuit City, Toys R Us, Big K, Pier 1, and more. No real surprises — just a good, down-home, "let's go to *the* mall for a day" experience. And don't forget to ride the giant carousel, the last fragment of what was once an amazing amusement park.

The **Lloyd Center** (2201 Lloyd Center, Sullivan's Gulch, 503-282-2511, www.lloydcentermall.com) is the granddaddy of Portland's malls. It's big and easily accessible by MAX, but there's nothing here you won't find in any mall in America. The food court is adequate and there is an ice chalet for recreation. The center has long been a fixture of life, not only in Portland, but also across the Northwest. It was one of the earliest gigantic shopping malls in the area and drew shopaholics from as far away as British Columbia — I know, because my mother-in-law was an early pioneer to the center. It's worth the pilgrimage for the sheer variety.

SECRET
SIDEWALKS

On sw Yamhill Street, between 3rd and 4th avenues, the sidewalk speaks. Engraved in the right-of-way are such sayings as "Famous last words," "Don't take any wooden nickels," "Here's looking at you, kid," "Now I've seen everything," "Shake a leg," "Wise crack," and, my favorite, "I never forget a face, but in your case I'll make an exception — Groucho Marx."

SECRET
SIMPSONS

Portland native Matt Groening (pronounced "gray-ning") changed television forever when he brought animation back to primetime with his immortal nuclear family, the Simpsons. With more than 300 episodes produced, *The Simpsons* has become the longest-running comedy on television as of this writing. Not only has creator Groening named

the Simpsons after his own family, many of the minor characters bear the names of streets in Portland, such as Quimby, Lovejoy, Terwilliger, and, of course, Flanders. The signs for NE Flanders Street are subject to more than their share of vandalism.

S E C R E T

SINISTER

Does everything have a dark side, even a hospital? The **Kaiser Permanente Clinic** in Rockwood (19500 SE Stark Street, Rockwood neighborhood, Gresham, Oregon, 503-669-3900, www.kaiser permanente.org) keeps a garden of common poisonous plants, designed to alert parents to the dangers of seemingly innocent backyard blossoms. Hmm, is this the place to find a little nightshade?

S E C R E T

SISTERS

Beginning in 1959, Portland began developing sister-city relationships around the globe. The very first sister city was Sapporo, Japan. Next came Guadalajara, Mexico, in 1983; Corinto, Nicaragua, in 1985; and Asheklon, Israel, and Ulsan, South Korea, in 1987. Three cities joined the list in 1988: Khabarovsk, Russia; Kaohsiung, Taiwan; and Suzhou, China. The latest addition to this wide-ranging group is Mutare, Zimbabwe, which became a sister city in 1991.

SECRET

SKATEBOARDING

Thrasher magazine dubbed Portland the "king of skate parks," and the city is working hard to become the epicenter of this extreme sport. The recently opened skate park at the base of the Steel Bridge (NW Everett Street and Naito Parkway, Old Town Chinatown) will complement the Burnside ramps for advanced skateboarders. The **Burnside Skatepark** (under the Burnside Bridge, Old Town Chinatown) is not a park, and it's a little seedy looking. Its location under a steel structure gives it a film noir atmosphere, but it has some of the best skateboard ramps around. Kids who wanted a place to skateboard built this park, and the city gave it a stamp of approval. If the park looks familiar, it may be because it has appeared in some Nintendo video games.

Skateboarding is illegal downtown and you will be ticketed if you are caught. Don't say I didn't tell you.

Just a little out of town is the **Newberg Skatepark** (1201 Blaine Street, Newberg, Oregon, 503-538-7454). It opened in July 2000 and has 27,330 square feet of super-smooth concrete. The park provides free helmets (you must wear one), but be prepared to carry your own first aid kit.

SECRET

SKATING

In Portland, it rains and it's hardly ever cold enough to create natural ice, but that doesn't stop the city's ice aficionados. Skating is not a new phenomenon to the city; people were gliding long before the sport became an icy-hot TV item. Skaters settle for indoor rinks, mostly in malls, of which there are plenty. There are also rinks for those who prefer wheels to blades.

Everyone's favorite trailer-trash princess, Tonya Harding, can still be found on the rink at the **Clackamas Town Center Ice Chalet** (1200 SE 82nd Avenue, Clackamas, Oregon, 503-786-6000). She practiced here before her Olympic downfall.

The **Lloyd Center Ice Rink** (Lloyd Center Mall, Sullivan's Gulch, 503-288-6073, www.lloydcenterice.com) was once covered only by the sky. If you have children to amuse and serious shopping to do, this is an ideal place to do both.

The largest rink in the Portland metro area is the **Valley Ice Arena** (Valley Plaza Shopping Center, Beaverton, Oregon, 503-297-2521). For more than 30 years, this ice rink has been a fixture at the shopping center.

The **Oaks Park Skating Rink** (Oaks Park, foot of SE Spokane Street, Sellwood-Moreland, 503-236-5722) has been a Portland roller-skating favorite since 1905, with its highly polished floors. An organ still plays music to skate by. You'll find lots of pairs gliding arm-in-arm, and only a few hell-on-wheels hotties.

SECRET

SKYSCRAPERS

Let's face it: with Mount Hood looming in the background, taller than anything man could manufacture, you may not notice that Portland has its share of tall and impressive architecture. In case you missed them, the tallest buildings are the **Wells Fargo Tower** (sw 5th Avenue and sw Columbia Street, Downtown), 40 stories and 546 feet; the us **Bancorp Tower** (sw 6th Avenue and Burnside Street, Downtown), 40 stories and 536 feet; and the **KOIN Tower** (sw 2nd Avenue and sw Columbia Street, Downtown), 35 stories and 509 feet.

SECRET

SLEEPS

The **Hotel Vintage Plaza** (422 sw Broadway, Downtown, 503-228-1212 or 800-263-2305, www.vintageplaza.com) is the place to stay if you are a wine lover. The hotel, which was built in 1894 and is on the National Register of Historic Places, has paid homage to Oregon wine by naming the rooms after various area vineyards. The décor has a vineyard theme and there are complimentary evening wine tastings. If your wallet can stand the strain, pop for a night in one of the bi-level suites with Japanese-style soaker tubs and spiral staircases.

The **Hotel deLuxe** (729 sw 15th Avenue, Downtown, 503-219-2094 or 866-986-8085, www.hoteldeluxeportland.com) is a set straight from the movies of the 1930s and 1940s — plush, a little bit art deco, a little bit sexy, and just a touch opulent. It will be easy to imagine you as the star in your own romantic moment. The hotel also features an excellent restaurant, Gracie's, and a dark, almost film noir bar, the Driftwood Room.

The newest kid on the block is the **Hotel Lucia** (400 SW Broadway, Downtown, 503-221-1717, www.hotellucia.com), most recently known as the Imperial Hotel. It was recently renovated, and the corner rooms are especially large. The hotel has all the best contemporary features, wifi, iPod docking stations, and my personal favorite — two bathrooms! Anyone who has ever waited, ahem, patiently, for their turn will adore this hotel. To make your life even easier there is a cocktail lounge (Bo's Restobar) and a Thai restaurant (Typhoon) on the ground floor. The only drawback is the 4 PM check-in, but they will hold your luggage while you go and explore the city.

The Pony Soldier (9901 NE Sandy Boulevard, Gresham, Oregon, 503-265-1504) is another hotel find. What's so secret about this Best Western? The warmth and service. Alan and Christine Crosby have been running the Pony Soldier for more than a decade. The staff members, who almost never seem to change, remember your name and go out of their way to be helpful. The generously sized rooms have microwaves, refrigerators, robes, irons, and comfy recliners for an end-of-the-day read. There is a pool and a hot tub, an exercise room, and a guest laundry. It's a little to the east of the city, but within two blocks of the MAX train. The Pony Soldier will also pick you up from the airport from 8 AM to 9 PM, if you call in advance.

Way at the other end of the economic scale is the **Hostelling-International Portland** (3031 SE Hawthorne Boulevard, at 30th Avenue, Sunnyside, 503-236-3380 or 866-447-3031, www.portlandhostel.org). This hostel is in a great location, near lots of cafés, shops, and nightlife.

SECRET

SNAKES

She's an exotic South American beauty. She doesn't like being messed with too much. She's Melba, a 12-foot-long, 62-pound green anaconda, and she's a new addition to the Oregon Zoo's Amazon Flooded Forest exhibit.

There's something truly awesome about anacondas, known in South America as "matatoros," or bull killers. They are almost mythical, particularly in their ability to glide underwater. So take a few moments to meet Melba. She'll probably be a bit bigger by the time you see her. Anacondas continue to grow over their lifetimes, sometimes reaching lengths of more than 25 feet.

SECRET

SNIFTERS

It may surprise you to discover that some of the world's finest eau de vie is made in Portland. Just north of the cafés and boutiques lining NW 23rd Avenue, **Clear Creek Distillery** (2389 NW Wilson Street, 503-248-9470, www.clearcreekdistillery.com) has been busy establishing itself as a contender in an industry dominated by international giants. Using local fruit, much of which is produced on his family farm, distiller Steve McCarthy turns out a variety of products, including whole pears in the bottle. And just how do they get a whole pear inside a bottle, you ask? The bottles are tied to tree limbs just after the tree flowers, allowing the pear to mature inside. I wonder if this is how they do the ship in a bottle?

S E C R E T

SNOBS
❖

Nestled into the base of Portland's west hills, Nob Hill is a sophisticated pocket of the city snuggled into the Northwest neighborhood. Sharing more than just a passing similarity with its San Francisco namesake, Nob Hill has undergone a revitalizing renaissance over the past decades. Victorian dwellings line the narrow streets, offering visitors a glimpse into the city's architectural past. Storefronts have been restored to their original splendor, transforming NW 23rd Avenue ("trendy-third" in local parlance) into a shopper's paradise. Dozens of whimsical, independent, and glamorous boutiques have opened, selling everything from tiaras to topiaries. There are restaurants, pubs, and cafés, some of which are open to the street on summer days. If you like Italian, check out **Caffe Mingo** and **Serrato** (see "Secret Italian"). And trees — oh, the trees. Unter den Linden in Berlin would be proud to call these trees its own. Nob Hill is a very special space in a city of special places.

SNOWSHOEING

Snowshoeing is a little more awkward than cross-country skiing, but it's gaining fast on the popularity track. Because it frequently uses the same tracks as cross-country skiing, the sport is beginning to boom. Portland doesn't get much snow, but just 45 miles out of town, Mount Hood has snow all year round. Give it a try — it's fun. You can rent snowshoes at the **Summit Ski Area** (54 miles east of Portland, on Highway 26, Government Camp, 503-272-0256).

SOLES

We can't help this entry — they make them here. **Niketown** (930 sw 6th Avenue, Downtown, 503-221-6453) is Portland's temple of running shoes. This state-of-the-art store showcases the very latest from the entire Nike line. If you're serious about your running shoes, you'll love this place. The clerks really know their stuff and can help fit you into a pair that will make you feel like an Olympic athlete in training. This store, however, is not where you go to find a bargain.

At the **Nike Factory Store** (2650 NE Martin Luther King, Jr., Boulevard, Eliot, 503-281-5901), you will find better prices with a lot less activity. There's even a mini Nike store in Portland International Airport, just in case you can't leave town without new shoes.

For a diagnostic fitting, go to **Pace Setter Athletic** (4306 SE

Woodstock Boulevard, Woodstock, 503-777-3214, www.pacesetter athletic.com). The staff will examine the way you've worn down your old shoes and make recommendations based on the shoe wear. Show your student identification and you'll qualify for a discount.

Can't resist just one more pair? **Imelda's** (3426 SE Hawthorne Boulevard, Sunnyside, 503-233-7476, www.imeldasandlouies.com) has shoes you'll seldom find in department or chain stores. Owner Pam Coven keeps a mix of well-heeled and definitely haute couture footwear in stock. You'll find more than shoes — handbags, jewelry, and hosiery round out the inventory.

SECRET
SPAS

Do your toes need a polish? Your skin a scrub? Can you just not go another moment without being mummified in seaweed? You won't have far to look. Spas are hot in Portland, particularly day spas.

Urbaca (120 NW 9th Avenue, Downtown, 503-241-5030) is an intimate spa retreat focusing on herbal wraps and aqua facelifts. The services are tailored to each customer and you'll find an array of exotic treatments to try.

Bellini's European Day Spa (2326 NW Irving Street, Northwest, 503-226-1526, bellinis.ypguides.net) has the more traditional treatments of facials, massage, and aromatherapy.

The **Aequis Spa** (422 NW 13th Avenue, 503-223-7847, www .aequisspa.com) is quite unlike any other spa in the city. It exists inside a not-so-chic warehouse behind an unmarked door (don't worry, you don't need a password). After ringing the silent bell (you'll have to trust me, it does ring), you're led down a candlelit hallway. Soothing music surrounds you and the staff speaks in hushed tones. The outside world ceases to exist. Aequis practices the science of Ayurveda, which originated in ancient India. A massage is much more than you would expect. It begins with a foot treatment. Then you choose essential oils to be used for your head-to-toe experience, which ends with a luxurious shower in a private bath. In all, it takes about two hours and costs about $150.

Dosha (2281 NW Glisan Street, Northwest, 503-228-8280) is the place to pamper yourself silly. The usual treatments are available — this was the first Aveda lifestyle spa on the West Coast — and all are performed with skill and flair. For the ultimate in pampering, Dosha offers a package that includes steam, a body wrap, massage, manicure, pedicure, hair styling, and cosmetic application for a mere $265. If that doesn't cure your jet lag, nothing will.

And, of course, Portland also has an **Aveda Lifestyle Store and Spa** (340 SW Morrison Street, 503-224-9339), with all its chi-chi services.

SECRET
SPEED
❀

Dream of being a Michael Andretti or Jacques Villeneuve? The **Pi-tarresi Pro Drive Racing School** (Portland International Raceway, 1940 N Victory Boulevard, Bridgeton, 503-285-4449, www.prodrive .net) might just start you on the road to that success — provided you're young, talented, and filled with endless energy.

For those who just want to watch the cars go zoom-zoom-zoom, the **Portland International Raceway** (1940 N Victory Boulevard, Bridgeton, 503-823-RACE, www.portlandraceway.com) has a full tank of events to keep the most devoted motorheads happy — everything from Champ Cars to go-karts zip around a very challenging road course. In June, during the Rose Festival, the big boys (CART) come to town for one of the première races of the season.

S E C R E T
SPORTS

With all Portland's beer, you've got to have sports. And in the Rose Quarter, Portlanders have them in profusion. Yes, they still envy Seattle's Mariners and Seahawks, but they've learned to live with what they have.

The **Portland Trail Blazers** (Rose Garden Arena, 1 N Center Court Street, Downtown, 503-234-9291, www.nba.com/blazers) are the NBA franchise in town. The team plays to mostly sellout crowds. The new **Portland Fire** are the Women's NBA addition to the Portland sports scene. You'll also find the **Portland Winter Hawks** (Memorial Coliseum, 300 Winning Way, Downtown, 503-238-6366), a Western Hockey League franchise that has nurtured such NHL superstars as Cam Neely.

The **Portland Beavers** (PGE Park, 1844 SW Morrison, Downtown, www.portlandbeavers.com) is the city's Triple A minor league baseball team. The Beavers play to a very enthusiastic crowd that keeps hope eternal that soon Portland will have its very own major league team to rival Seattle's.

SECRET

SPORTS BARS

When you just have to cheer on your favorite team and you need some help, there's nothing like the company at a sports bar (even if most of the crowd is rooting for the wrong side). **Claudia's** (3006 SE Hawthorne Boulevard, Sunnyside, 503-232-1744, www.claudiaspub .com) is possibly Portland's best sports pub. A healthy crowd almost every night fills the high-backed swivel captain's chairs at the bar. The chairs are a wonderful addition, allowing you to turn and watch the action on one of many TV sets showing half a dozen games. If you don't want to be quite so sedentary, there are pool tables. Good, simple pub food is what you'll find here — nothing exotic.

The regulars at the **Skybox Pub & Grill** (7995 SE Milwaukie Avenue, Sellwood-Moreland, 503-731-6399) are not going to be at all happy that I've let you in on their favorite spot, but I just couldn't resist. Skybox has mastered the art of pub grub. You'll need both hands and lots of napkins for the juicy burgers. Crinkle-cut French fries are a must — try them with ranch dressing. The Skybox is smoke-free and child friendly. Surprisingly, even when it's busy, it's not crowded. The owners, Jim Hughes and Dennis Vigna, seem to know everyone and they make it a point to introduce themselves to newcomers. You see, TV bars aren't the only place you can go where everybody knows your name.

At the **Cheerful Tortoise** (1939 SW 6th Avenue, Downtown, 503-224-3377), students from Portland State University and the after-work crowd from Downtown gather to watch a game on one of the 20 televisions (two of which are satellite). What's the draw? Nearly 20 beers on tap, a huge menu of cheap food, and, on Thursday nights, $1 draft beers. Of course it's going to be packed. Be prepared to be up close and personal with your fellow sports fans.

The Agency (1939 sw Morrison Street, Downtown, 503-548-2921, www.theagencyentertainment.com), located close to PGE Park, bills itself as "the ultimate sports bar." It certainly is shiny and bright with enough television sets to keep the most devout sports fan occupied for many an hour.

S E C R E T

SQUARE DANCING

Square dancing — it's not just for cowgirls anymore. These days you'll find everyone from computer engineers to nurses do-si-dohing up a storm. The **Aloha Grange** (3425 sw 185th Avenue, Beaverton, Oregon, 503-848-9839) is filled with dancers in full regalia: men in Western shirts and Stetsons, and women in short, full, twirling skirts. Free lessons are held perodically, so be sure to call and see if classes are available while you are visiting. Based on a form of the French quadrille, square dancing is now popular around the world.

S E C R E T

SQUARES

Whatever you do, or however limited your schedule, take the time to lounge for a bit in Portland's living room — **Pioneer Courthouse**

Square (sw Broadway and sw Morrison Street, Downtown). The city's first public school once occupied this site, as did a magnificent hotel. Then the site was turned into an eyesore of a parking lot. When the city decided to turn the square into a public space, it launched a very clever marketing campaign: it asked citizens to buy the bricks needed to create the square. The bricks bear the names of the contributors, and almost all of the 45,000 needed were sold. The square hosts political rallies, rock concerts, flower shows, and, of course, a daily parade that's great for people-watching.

On the lower level of the square is the TriMet office (an excellent place to buy transit passes) and sparkling clean and safe public restrooms. Up above, next to the Starbucks, is the **Weather Machine**, which announces the meteorological conditions at noon every day with a spray of mist and a fanfare of trumpets (see "Secret Weather").

And, of course, there is the **Courthouse**, a sturdy but still graceful historic building. There's a post office on the first floor, and from the cupola you can snap some great photos of the city. To get to the cupola, take the elevator to the third floor, turn left, go through the door, and walk up two flights. As security procedures constantly change, the cupola may or may not be open to the public.

"**Fareless Square**" (information at the Portland Oregon Visitors Association, 1000 sw Broadway, Suite 2300, Downtown, 503-275-9750, www.travelportland.com) is the downtown area where you can hop on and off the MAX, vintage trolleys, and streetcars for absolutely nothing (see "Secret Free Rides").

S E C R E T

STOGIES

"A woman is only a woman, but a good cigar is a smoke." It's a memorable line, attributed in various sources either to Edward G. Robinson in *The Whole Town's Talking* or to Rudyard Kipling. Whoever said it, many share the sentiment.

Rich's Cigar Store (820 sw Alder Street, Downtown, 503-228-1700, www.richscigar.com) is the place to stock up on stogies and get the news from home. This is one of the few Portland emporiums stocking out-of-town newspapers and magazines.

The **Cascade Cigar Store** (9691 SE 82nd Avenue, Happy Valley, 800-593-4123, www.cascadecigar.com) has been lighting up people's lives for more than 45 years. Walk into the onsite humidor and experience the aromas of 1,200 square feet of wall-to-wall cigars. Macanudo, Arturo Fuente (including the Fuente Opus x), Padron, Ashton, and Partagas, as well as many boutique brands, are all in stock. Did you know that cigars are best kept in a 70/70 environment (70 degrees Fahrenheit and 70 percent humidity)? That's why a cigar shop needs a humidor, unless all the customers are taking the merchandise home to some steamy climate.

The Cascade sells more than cigars. This is tobacco central for pipe smokers, too. In fact, the store invites you to bring in your pipe and sample some of the more than 100 pipe blends in stock. There are accessories, too: tobacco cases, reamers, tampers, and, of course, pipe cleaners.

SECRET

STONE

The **Founders' Stone** (Governor Tom McCall Waterfront Park) honors Portland's founders, William Pettygrove and Asa Lovejoy, who
tossed a coin to decide whether their new town would be named
Boston or Portland. To see that penny, visit the Oregon History
Center (see "Secret History").

SECRET

STREETCARS

Portland is perhaps the most forward-thinking city in the nation
when it comes to public transport. Portland was the first city in the
United States to introduce modern, European-style streetcars to its
roadways (www.portlandstreetcar.org). Made in the Czech Republic, the air-conditioned cars run 18 hours a day over a 2.5-mile line
stretching from northwest Portland to the downtown campus of
Portland State University. The streetcars stop by Powell's City of
Books in The Pearl, the Central Library, and the Portland Art Museum,
as well as a slew of shops. Talk about user friendly!

Streetcars are not new to the city. At one time, Portland had more
than 200 miles of streetcar tracks, and cars shuttled citizens around
the city. Bringing back the streetcars is a good way to start repairing
the damage done by ripping up all those miles of tracks to make way
for the automobile empire.

Portlanders take their transit system very seriously. So seriously that you may want to visit www.trimettiquette.com, the city's answer to how Miss Manners would ride the Max train and streetcars. You'll find the "unofficial" but socially important rules on how to be a better passenger, including: shower, smoke outside the bus shelter even when it's raining, and don't sit down next to someone when there are empty pairs of seats — even if they are cute. Make that *especially* if they are cute.

SECRET
STREET CORNERS

A crossroads can truly define a city or a neighborhood. For a look at the varied personality of Portland, try hanging out on one of these street corners:

NW **23rd Avenue and** NW **Kearney Street** is the center of the "trendy-third" district. Shops, bistros, and lots of espresso flavor this bustling junction.

SE **37th Avenue and** SE **Hawthorne Boulevard** is where New Age meets Old Age (the '60s hippie years). Candles, incense, pizza, beer, tattoos, and, of course, coffee all snuggle up side by side in one the city's liveliest neighborhoods.

This one you have to see to believe. It's a neighborhood experiment in "intersection repair" by the local residents. The corner of SE **9th Avenue and** SE **Sherrett Street** sports a tea stand, a book lending station, and a revolving art project.

SE **Milwaukie Avenue and** SE **Bybee Street**, the heart of the

Sellwood antique district, has a "main street" feel. You could spend all day just exploring the four different corners.

SECRET

SURFING

Portland is only two hours at most from the ocean, so you'll find it easy to discover one of the state's better-kept secrets — it's an ideal place to surf! Much of Oregon's northern coast, from Lincoln City north, is protected as state parks or public beaches. It's a divine location to camp. You'll wake up in the morning to the sight of waves, free of too many surfboards. You would be wise to bring a wetsuit for these chillier climes; the ocean can be downright icy at times.

SECRET

SWEAT

Portland's climate is temperate, temperate, temperate, which means you're not going to find much air conditioning. However, July and August will see some days that hit the 90-degree mark. Don't try to do *all* your sightseeing in one day, carry a water bottle, and slow down.

S E C R E T

TASTINGS

It's lovely to spend a weekend in the wine country west of city, but if you need a wine fix right now, several places in town will quell that craving.

Just a handful of stools at the bar and a couple of cozy tables are all you will find for seating at **Oregon Wines on Broadway** (515 sw Broadway, Downtown, 503-228-4655, www.oregonwinesonbroadway .com). This diminutive establishment is the best place in town to learn about Oregon wines. On almost any given night, you'll find at least 30 Oregon Pinot Noirs available by the glass, and a good assortment of white wines.

The bar of the **Southpark Seafood Grill & Wine Bar** (901 sw Salmon Street, Downtown, 503-326-1300) would look perfectly at home in a 19th-century Paris salon. The high ceilings, long heavy drapes, and mural give it a very romantic air. It's the perfect place for sipping champagne or any other wine you'd like to try by the glass.

If you happen to be staying at the **Hotel Vintage Plaza** (422 sw Broadway, Downtown, 503-228-1212), you'll be treated to a complimentary tasting of Northwest wines every evening in the lobby.

Gregg Fujino, one of Portland's most astute and friendly wine sellers, runs **Woodstock Wine & Deli** (4030 se Woodstock Boulevard, Woodstock, 503-777-2208). Woodstock takes the tasks of tasting, cataloging, and researching wines very seriously — but don't worry, you'll still have fun at the tastings. Since there's a deli attached, tastings sometimes last well into the evenings.

Wine lovers can also find information on Oregon wines at www
.oregonwine.com.

S E C R E T

TAX
⚜

Since there is no sales tax in Oregon, Portland is a shopper's heaven.
Canadians used to come here in flocks larger than those of Canada geese
when the two currencies were closer in value. Hordes of Washington
residents still regularly invade the city on shopping expeditions.

On the other hand, there is a sneaky little tax on rental cars, but
only at the airport. If you can arrange to pick up your car somewhere
other than PDX, such as Beaverton or Hillsboro, you'll avoid the
11-percent airport concession fee and the 12.5-percent Multnomah
County tax that applies at both the airport and downtown Portland
car rental offices.

Not to throw too much cold water on your tax-free spending spree,
but don't forget that hotel rooms in Portland charge a 11.5-percent
occupancy tax.

S E C R E T

TAXIS
⚜

Because Portland is a fairly compact city, getting around by taxi
can be reasonably economical. Finding a taxi is the problem. Unlike

New York, Portland doesn't let you just step to the curb and whistle. The best place to grab a cab in a hurry is to go to one of the major hotels, or phone for one. **Broadway Cab** (503-227-1234) and **Radio Cab** (503-227-1212) both offer 24-hour radio-dispatched service and accept most major credit cards.

SECRET

TEA
❧

According to Chinese legend, it was Emperor Shen Nung who discovered tea by accident in 2737 BC, when a few leaves of tea fell into water he was boiling to drink. He drank the mixture, enjoying the newfound taste, and thus the long history of tea began. We've come a long way, baby. Now there are more than 3,000 variations of tea, which will carry us well into the new millennium.

How did tea drinking in the afternoon come about? Tradition has it that afternoon tea was begun in 1840 in England by Anna, the seventh duchess of Bedford. Dinner was served quite late, and in summer there was a particularly long interval between lunch and the evening meal. Anna experienced a "sinking feeling" in the afternoons, so she ordered her servants to send up snacks, accompanied by tea. As the duchess's friends joined her in this practice, the ritual of afternoon tea became fashionable. Ah, the good old days.

Okay, admit it, sometimes you drink tea in a Starbucks coffeehouse. In Portland, that's quite okay, because **Tazo** tea is created here. It all began quite simply in Steven Smith's kitchen in 1994. When he had a blend with which he was satisfied, he began to market it to local establishments — in pickle jars. The first, a fruit blend, was called "Simply Red." Smith's hard work paid off; in 1999, Starbucks purchased Tazo. But Tazo reflects only one aspect of the tea phenomenon in the city.

In Portland, the **Tao of Tea** (239 NW Everett Street, Sunnyside, 503-224-8455, www.taooftea.com) is the last word in tea emporiums. Here, tea is a very serious and sensual business. Even the kind of cup you drink your beverage from will depend upon what kind of tea you order. Relax. Put yourself in the tea master's hands and sink into a cozy room bedecked with colorful cushions.

The Tea Zone (510 NW 11th Avenue, 503-221-2130, www.teazone .com), tucked into a side street of The Pearl neighborhood, is a discreet place to kick back with a book and a fine cup of oolong or one of 49 other varieties of tea. The selection is eclectic, with leaves ranging from Asian varieties to South American yerba matés. At the Tea Zone, you will learn about body (the tea's flavor and strength), fannings (a very small leaf, usually used in teabags), and tips (the very end of the delicate buds, considered to be the most flavorful part of the plant). Hint: Green teas should be steeped in water of 160 to 175 degrees Fahrenheit, as boiling water may make the tea bitter.

S E C R E T

TEA CEREMONIES

Inside the small room, with its tatami floor and shoji sides, the only sounds are the muffled bubbling of the iron kettle and the hissing of a bamboo whisk in a teapot. A Japanese tea ceremony is in progress, continuing a tradition that dates back to the 16th century. Japan's *chado*, or way of tea, takes its style from an era when samurai warriors were required to remove their swords, out of respect, when entering a tearoom. Today there are few swords in evidence, but tea ceremony participants still enter a traditional tearoom through a tiny door. The **Wakai Tea Room** (see "Secret Japanese"), operated by the Wakai Dokokai, is open to the public on the last Tuesday of each month. Guests drink green tea and learn about the traditions. Cost is about $10–15.

At the **Japanese Garden** (see "Secret Japanese"), tea ceremonies are held on the third Saturday of every month from May through September. The gardens lend an unequaled authenticity to the occasion. Guests are only allowed to watch, not to participate. Cost is $6.

For a much less formal, although equally enjoyable, ceremony, visit the **Tao of Tea** (3430 SE Belmont Street, 503-736-0198, www .taooftea.com). Order one of the oolong varieties and you will be served not just a pot of tea, but an entire tray of tea-making equipment, including a miniature pot, cooling cups, tiny drinking cups, and a brazier and kettle. The shop's hostess will be happy to show you how to use the accessories, but after the initial instruction, you are on your own.

A warning: After experiencing these tea ceremonies, it's going to be hard to look your lowly mug and tea bag in the eye again.

SECRET
TENNIS

Love-15. Love-30. Love-40. No, this isn't romance through the ages. It's tennis. And soggy climate or not, there are plenty of places to play the game in Portland. Open to the public, the **Portland Tennis Center** (324 NE 12th Avenue, Kerns, 503-823-3189, www.pdx10s .com) has four indoor courts (two with ball machines) and eight outdoor courts. Reservations are necessary for the indoor courts and cost about $24 for a one-hour, fifteen-minute court time. The outdoor courts are free. The whole facility is run by the City of Portland.

For tennis in a forested setting, try **Mount Tabor Park**'s courts (see "Secret Volcanoes"). Three courts are near the reservoir and two more are on the west side of the park. All are open to the public.

If you want to stop and smell the roses between sets, head for Washington Park, where a number of the courts sit next to the **International Rose Test Garden** (see "Secret Gardens"). The views from here are magnificent, so it might be difficult to keep your mind on the game. But the scenery will make your wait for a court a little more enjoyable — and on sunny weekends, these play spaces are packed.

SECRET

THAI

Khun Pic's Bahn Thai (3429 SE Belmont Street, Sunnyside, 503-235-1610) has perhaps the best Thai food in the city. The chef waits until you place your order, and then makes it from scratch. It's a sweet little place, tucked away in a house, decorated with orchids and Thai items. Expect a wait because the service can be slow. A husband-and-wife team runs the restaurant.

Beautiful presentations are a highlight of **Sweet Basil Thai Cuisine**

(3135 NE Broadway, Sullivan's Gulch, 503-281-8337, www.sweetbasilor .com). It's good food at a good price. Try the roast duck with red curry or the panang seafood with pineapple fried rice. Whatever you select, it will be a visual treat.

The **Bangkok Kitchen** (2534 SE Belmont Street, Sunnyside, 503-236-7349) is a no-frills Thai restaurant that serves up the basics of Southeast Asian cookery. Hot-and-sour soups, aromatic curries, and tangy noodles are just a few of the menu staples. The soup orders are very large, so bring a few friends for the meal. A house specialty is the sea bass, whole and crisp in a concentrated chili sauce (bring your own fire extinguisher).

S E C R E T

THEATERS

Portland is theater mad. Not only do citizens flock to the **Portland Center for Performing Arts** (1111 SW Broadway, Downtown, 503-248-4335, www.pcpa.com), but they also support many private theater companies and facilities. The PCPA includes three buildings that house a total of four theaters: the Keller Auditorium, the Arlene Schnitzer Concert Hall, the Newmark Theatre, and the Dolores Winningstad Theatre.

The Keller Auditorium, known for its excellent acoustics and sight-lines, hosts the big stuff: the touring Broadway shows, ballets, and grand operas. Its resident companies include the Portland Opera, the Oregon Ballet Theater, and the Oregon Children's Theater.

The Arlene Schnitzer Concert Hall is noted for its Italian Rococo Revival architecture and is on the National Register of Historic Places. The hall houses the world's largest electronic organ, originally built for Carnegie Hall. Locals affectionately refer to this hall as "the Schnitz."

Antoinette Hatfield Hall (formerly the New Theatre building) opened in 1987 and houses the Newmark Theatre, designed for dramatic productions in an Edwardian style, and the Dolores Winningstad Theatre, patterned after a Shakespearean courtyard.

Ah, but there's more. **Portland Center Stage** (www.pcs.org), originally a branch of the Oregon Shakespeare Festival, began operating independently in 1994. It now uses the Gerding Theater at the Armory (128 NW 11th Avenue, 503-445-3700) for its presentations.

The **Artists Repertory Theatre** (1516 SW Morrison Street, Downtown, 503-241-1278, www.artistsrep.org) is a professional, not-for-profit theater company dedicated to challenging both artists and audiences with deep, provocative plays.

The **Miracle Theatre Group** (425 SE 6th Avenue, 503-236-7253, www.milagro.org) is the largest Hispanic arts and culture organization in the Pacific Northwest.

SECRET
THURSDAYS

On the **First Thursday** of each month, the galleries of The Pearl open their doors to show off their collections (www.firstthursday portland.com). This is one of the city's "oh so trendy" regular events that hints that Portland wants to be more than just beer and boats. If you're lucky enough to attend on a clear evening, you'll find a variety of artists hawking their wares on the street. Come gaze and browse, and be one of the sleek, pretty people for a night.

While First Thursday is a citywide happening, the heart of this event is definitely in The Pearl, centered on NW 13th Avenue and Glisan Street. Many galleries are clustered in old former warehouses. If you plan to have dinner in The Pearl before you begin your gallery quest, make a reservation well in advance. All the local bars and restaurants will be packed to the rafters.

Aside from the galleries in The Pearl, the Downtown core has a baker's dozen of galleries that have operated since the late 1970s or early 1980s. Most of these galleries are near the MAX line.

And then there's **Last Thursday**, the northeast Portland counterpart to the more upscale galleries of the Pearl. The 1400 to 2200 blocks of NE Alberta and Alameda Streets have a collection of local upcoming artists in galleries that are also up and coming. This is the place to find a burgeoning artist at a budget price. A favorite is **Shades of Color Gallery** (1476 NE Alberta Street, King, 503-288-5877).

S E C R E T

TOURS

❧

ART: **The Cultural Bus** (aka TriMet Bus 63) hits all the city's cultural hot spots, including the Portland Art Museum, the Oregon History Center, OMSI, and the Oregon Zoo. Local artist Henk Pander and his sons, Arnold and Jacob, designed the artwork on the bus.

The ART trip is itself a masterpiece. What makes this tour special is the price — the same as any TriMet fare. Since your transfer has a time stamp, you can hop off and on the bus as many times as you like, provided you are back on the bus before your transfer expires.

For more than 25 years, schoolchildren and adults have been learning local history from the volunteers of the **Urban Tour Group** (503-227-5780). Private tours cost $5 per person and reservations must be made in advance. You can choose from one of three stock tours, or have one tailored just for you.

SECRET

TOYS
❀

They don't make them like this anymore, but you can rediscover some favorites of your childhood, and your grandfather's childhood, at the **Kidd Toy Museum** (1301 SE Grand Avenue, Buckman, 503-233-7807). A vast collection of toys, mostly dolls and cast-iron pieces, is displayed throughout three buildings. It's quite a change from the stuff kids are into these days, but they'll enjoy seeing what used to be considered state of the art. Everything is at least 50 to 150 years old.

Oh, you wanted something to buy and take home? No problem. **Finnegan's Toys and Gifts** (922 SW Yamhill Street, Downtown, 503-221-0306, www.finneganstoys.com) is the biggest and best toy store in the city. It's a great place to keep a small one enthralled (and older ones, too). Part of the store has been set aside for "test drives" of windup cars, flip-over monkeys, and other moving toys. There are all kinds of board games, dollhouses, and dress-up clothes, and a really good selection of puppets and stuffed animals.

Tammie's Hobbies (12024 sw Canyon Road, Sylvan-Highland, 503-644-4535, www.tammieshobbies.com) is one of the few stores that carries German LGB train sets and their spare parts. You'll also find radio-controlled race cars, airplanes, and boats. In fact, there are models of all sorts and sizes, a paint center, and a full range of paintball supplies for those weekend warrior outings.

SECRET
TRANSIT STOPS
❧

Is it an indoor/outdoor gallery? A museum? Or simply the best use of public funds in a long, long time? It's art on the MAX lines. Through the Westside MAX Public Art Program, artists' visions and works were added to the design of the light-rail stops. For the cost of a ride — a mere pittance — you can view some of the most innovative art the city has to offer. And, best of all, you don't walk your feet off going from gallery to gallery — the train rolls you from one exhibit to the next!

Starting in Portland, at the PGE **Park** stop, the design team used the buildings and plaza to express the importance of oratory in the city's history. Bronze podiums invite spontaneous speakers and punctuation marks form seating and accents on the Yamhill platform.

At **Kings Hill**, the team acknowledged the neighborhood's history with a test about Tanner Creek embedded in the brick sidewalk.

Goose wings stretch across the protective canopy at **Goose Hollow**. When the sun shines, buildings in the glass line up with the "street."

The design team took inspiration from geology at the **Washington Park** station. A core sample of the drilling for this location was used to form a "timeline." Circular stools mimic the core samples and light boxes shimmer with fossil-like images.

At the **Beaverton Transit Center**, photographer Barbara Gilson and students from the C.E. Mason Arts and Communications High School collaborated on a series of photos to decorate the stop. Humorous portraits express styles of waiting, local landmarks appear as snapshots, and a "time window" documents the 1994 landscape.

Beaverton Creek is a truly stellar experience. Artist Anne Connell designed this as a navigation station. Passengers can mark time and contemplate the universe with a 24-hour clock and a map of the solar system. Stars are arranged in constellations. Two compass roses indicate true north. And brick patterns suggest borders on an old map.

At **Willow Creek**, you can imagine yourself reading under cherry trees. "Living room" furniture has been sandblasted with authors' names, literary characters are hidden in puzzles, and letters from the world's alphabets are scattered in the concrete. Bricks are used to recall falling cherry blossoms.

The design team drew inspiration from the natural world at **Quatama**. Here, a river-like path includes boulders with scientific images and a basin showing the mechanics of rainwater run-off. Animal tracks cross the platform and artist Michael Oppenheimer's *Cattail Tunes* sways with the wind.

The **Fair Complex/Hillsboro Airport** stop celebrates the spirit of achievement. An ivy-covered trophy boasts "The World's Greatest" (you can fill in the blank any way you like), photographs from past fairs decorate the glass, and historic model airplanes spin over an aerial-view landscape.

Three hundred bronze swallows accompany a Shakespeare quote (no, I'm not going to tell you which one — ride the train and find out) and swallow weathervanes top the shelters at the **Tuality Hospital** stop.

At the **Hillsboro Central** stop, photographs and bronze objects celebrate local heritage. A letter from the 1870s has been etched into the shelter glass and the weathervane recalls bygone train signals.

The **Hatfield Government Center** is the end of the line, and here the theme is gathering and dispersal (ooh, how governmental). A scarecrow weathervane fends off crows above the shelter. Trackside granite balls appear to roll out of bronze baskets, and a sculpted bronze rail features local plants and products.

And you thought all you would get for the price of a ticket was a ride.

SECRET

TURKEY

Is there anything as comforting as a turkey dinner with all the trimmings? Who cares if it's not November; there are times you need a turkey dinner just like Mom used to make. Head for **Huber's** (411 SW 3rd Street, Downtown, 503-228-5686, www.hubers.com), the oldest restaurant in Portland. It first opened its doors in 1879 and has rarely closed them since. You'll have to look carefully for this restaurant, as it's tucked inside the Oregon Pioneer Building, down a hallway. The main room has a vaulted stained-glass ceiling and mahogany paneling. Even the original brass cash register is on-scene. But let's talk turkey. You can order a classic turkey dinner — it's the house specialty — or turkey enchiladas, turkey Parmesan, even turkey Morocco. You get the point. This is turkey heaven, so gobble away.

SECRET
TZATZIKI

Creamy tzatziki, possibly the best in the Northwest, is a specialty of **Berbati** (19 sw 2nd Avenue, Downtown, 503-226-2122, www .berbati.com). But don't stop with the tzatziki. Order up a whole table of appetizers, such as the delicious dolmades or tangy tiropita. The Greek salads are both authentic and unadulterated (no potato salad hiding in the bottom here). If you have room, try the calamari or chicken souvlaki; both will have you dancing to the rhythms of Zorba the Greek. Did I mention dancing? Next door is Berbati's Pan, bustling with live music. The atmosphere here is noisy and noisy. But if you can stand the din, you'll be well rewarded with a dinner to remember.

SECRET
VALENTINES

Beer and chocolate: it's just what you would expect from Portland, the epicenter of microbreweries on the West Coast. Every year on

Valentine's Day, the **Dublin Pub** (6821 sw Beaverton Highway, Raleigh Hills neighborhood, Beaverton, Oregon, 503-297-2889, www.dublinpubpdx.com) offers up "Fred Eckhardt's Chocolate and Beer Tasting." Eckhardt claims to have invented the pairing when he accidentally dropped a partially eaten chocolate bar into his tumbler of ale. Not one to waste, Fred downed the beer and "discovered" a new taste. The latest tasting paired 10 beers with 10 chocolates, and included warm-up and cool-down pints. Beer. It's not just for breakfast anymore.

S E C R E T
VIDEOS

Mike Clark's Movie Madness (4320 SE Belmont Street, Sunnyside, 503-234-4363, www.moviemadnessvideo.com) is one of the best independent video stores in the United States. You can roam through aisles of new releases, cult films, classics, foreign movies, art films, independent films, and, yes, some DVDs. The store specializes in hard-to-find videos. Lift your eyes from the titles from time to time to spot such items as props from *Pulp Fiction* and *Star Wars*, the hat Tony Curtis wore in *Some Like It Hot*, and the prop knife used in the shower scene in *Psycho*.

Trilogy (2325 NW Thurman Street, Northwest, 503-229-1884, www .trilogy-video.com) claims to have the best selection of international films in the city. Movies such as *The Road Home* from China and *Orfeu* from Brazil are just two in the vast selection.

SECRET

VIETNAMESE

For a West Coast city, Portland is surprisingly short on really good Chinese restaurants. The Vietnamese have taken up the slack with scores of places to eat really good Asian food. However, Vietnamese restaurants tend to change locations almost as fast as people change their socks. So call ahead, because a great place yesterday may not be there tomorrow.

Thai PK Restaurant (6141 sw Macadam Avenue, Lair Hill, 503-452-4396) offers an extensive menu of standard Vietnamese dishes. Keeping with the time-honored custom of Asian restaurants, Thai PK starts with complimentary soup. Try not to slurp down too much — this is only a starter. Leave room for miang kum (spinach leaves stuffed with dried shrimp, peanuts, and coconut) or pad thai that's not too sticky or sweet.

Thien Hong (6749 NE Sandy Boulevard, Roseway, 503-281-1247) can make you like — no, love — squid. It arrives atop a formidable mound of greens and sliced onion and is perfectly cooked: peppery, spicy, and crisp, not greasy. The spring rolls are excellent and the braised duck with curry noodles gives your taste buds a punch. In all, there are about 130 choices on the menu, so you may have to revisit this establishment a few times.

S E C R E T

VINES
❖

On weekends, many Portlanders head for the hills, or at least to the undulating elevations of the Willamette Valley, to saunter through and sample the vineyards. Many varieties of grapes are grown in Oregon, but Pinot Noir is the state's signature grape. The Willamette Valley is an ideal location to grow grapes. The valley sits on the same latitude as France's Burgundy wine region.

The vineyards are remarkably close to the city, some only 20 minutes south of the downtown area. Many of these vineyards are small, especially by California standards, but most are open daily for tasting and onsite sales. The area between Newberg and McMinnville is considered the center of the wine region.

Oregon's wines are delicate and fruity. Pinot Noir, Chardonnay, Riesling, and Cabernet Sauvignon are the most common varietals. There are also many fruit wines, such as blackberry, raspberry, boysenberry, loganberry, and plum.

Route 99, the state's official Wine Highway, heads west toward McMinnville and will bring you close to most of the wineries.

About 20 miles southwest of Portland, near the town of Newberg, **Rex Hill** (30835 N Route 99w, Newberg, Oregon, 503-538-0666 or 800-739-4455, www.rexhill.com) produces consistently fine Pinot Noir wines. The site was formerly a 20-acre fruit farm with a brick nut-drying plant. The plant was rebuilt into the nucleus of the winery, with the former drying caves intact. The tasting room is open daily from 11 AM to 5 PM. Tours are by appointment only.

Duck Pond Cellars (23145 Route 99w at Fox Farm Road, Newberg,

Oregon, 503-538-3199 or 800-437-3213, www.duckpondcellars.com) opened in 1993. It's open by appointment only from January to Memorial Day. During the summer, there are tours on Wednesdays, Fridays, Saturdays, and Sundays, at 12 noon and 2 PM.

The **Ponzi Vineyards Winery** (14665 sw Winery Lane, Beaverton, Oregon, 503-628-1277, www.ponziwines.com) is open daily from 10 AM to 5 PM. It specializes in Pinot Noir, Pinot Gris, and Chardonnay. The intimate tasting room overlooks the original estate vineyard, one of the oldest in the Willamette Valley. Current releases are available for tasting. Private tours are held for groups of five or more only, and cost $10 per person. The fee does include a tasting of the current wines, accompanied by crackers and imported cheeses. In 1988, the *Wine Advocate* recognized winemaker Richard Ponzi as one of the top 15 international winemakers.

Wineries and vineyards are scattered all over the Willamette Valley. For a complete list, try www.oregonwine.com or pick up a copy of *Oregon Wine* magazine. Better yet, just head out onto Route 99 and stop where your nose takes you.

S E C R E T

VINTAGE CLOTHING

Once upon a time, we looked for "old" clothing in charity shops run by the Junior League or a hospital volunteer corps, or perhaps on the rack at Goodwill or the Salvation Army. Now, entire stores are devoted to the clothes we turned up our noses at in our grandmothers' closets. Turns out they had more style than we gave them credit for.

The **Buffalo Exchange** (1420 SE 37th Avenue, Sunnyside, 503-234-1302; and 1036 W Burnside, 503-222-3418, www.buffaloexchange .com) is a secondhand store that works hard to be not merely secondhand, but also vintage. The store, which began as a small shop in Tucson, Arizona, will recycle your used goods, too, but don't expect any payment for them. This is a great last-minute stop when your wallet is thin and you have a yen for something special.

Decades Vintage Company (328 SW Stark Street, Downtown, 503-223-1177, www.decadesvintage.com) carries a full line of men's and women's vintage — not thrift shop — fashion. The specialty is clothing from the 1930s to the 1970s, and many of the items have never been worn. If you've watched a classic movie and swooned over an Audrey Hepburn or Lauren Bacall look, this is the place to begin searching out that style. It's hip and retro simultaneously. You can outfit yourself with a classic blazer and a funky hand-painted tie, or a vintage Pendleton wool skirt and a Hawaiian shirt — please, don't wear them together!

The Red Light Clothing Exchange (3590 SE Hawthorne Boulevard, Sunnyside, 503-963-8888, www.redlightclothingexchange.com) has recycled items for both men and women. An especially good place for skinny, budget-minded fashionistas.

Hundreds of glittery party dresses and gowns hang in chronological order in **Ray's Ragtime** (1001 SW Morrison Street, Downtown, 503-226-2616). There's also an excellent collection of costume jewelry, tons of men's suits and ties, and Hawaiian and bowling shirts (if they haven't all been snapped up by bargain-hunting Californians).

SECRET
VOLCANOES

Mount Tabor Park (SE 60th Avenue and SE Salmon Street, Mount Tabor, 503-823-2525, www.portlandonline.com/parks/) is the only volcano within city limits in the 48 continental states. From the summit, you'll gaze out on one of the finer views of Portland's west hills and Mount Hood. Tabor was named in honor of the twin peaks in Palestine. The park appeals to a wide range of city dwellers, including hikers, dog lovers, joggers, and skateboarders. Look out for the pavement lugers who hurtle down the streets at lightning speed, especially on Wednesdays, when the park is closed to automobile traffic.

Need a sunset viewpoint for a picnic? Mount Tabor is an excellent choice. Picnic above the reservoir on the west side and watch the sun slide below the Portland hills.

And how many parks do you know that come with a natural amphitheater? In the remnant of the volcano crater, you'll find just such a theater waiting for productions.

Just a few miles north of Portland is probably the most famous volcano of recent years — **Mount St. Helens**. This now flat-topped mountain blew its stack in May 1980. When it was finished, it was 1,300 feet shorter. The force of its eruption has been compared to 500 times the force of the Hiroshima blast. The landslide that accompanied the blast was the largest ever recorded. If you aren't fortunate enough to fly over the volcano on your way into the city, then by all means drive the distance to see this sight. The crater left by the eruption is more than a mile wide and draws nearly 600,000 visitors a year.

Follow I-5 north for about 40 minutes and take the Castle Rock exit, then go east on the Spirit Lake Memorial Highway. At the base of the ridge is Cinedome, a three-story-high theater with a 55-foot-wide screen. The only movie that plays is the Academy Award–nominated film *The Eruption of Mount St. Helens*. You'll experience the bone-rattling sound of the eruption. Drive on to the visitors' center at Silver Lake to view hundreds of historical photos, geological surveys, and many other exhibits. A second visitors' center sits atop Cold Water Ridge. The view from here can only be described as spectacular. You'll see the remains of the crater, the debris-filled valley of the Toutle River, and the new lakes formed by the massive mudslides.

The blast scalded at least 150,000 acres surrounding the mountain. The Silver Lake Center focuses on the biological recovery of the landscape. The recovery has been amazing. Both flora and fauna have returned to the area much faster than scientists anticipated.

The area is not yet filled with hotels, but there is the quirky little **Tent and Breakfast** (14000 Spirit Lake Highway Toutle, Washington) in the blow-down area. You'll sleep in roomy wall tents, and eat a chuck-wagon dinner and breakfast beside the lake. It's a little pricey at $150 per person or $285 per couple. But hey — how often do you get to sleep beside an almost-dormant volcano?

If you can't make it to the mountain, you can still take a photograph from the meditation room at The Grotto (see "Secret Grotto"). On clear days, this room offers perhaps the best long-distance view of Mount St. Helens to be had within the city limits.

My favorite view remains a pair of photos of my parents' home. One was taken with the mountain in the background and the other the day after the mountain blew its top — no mountain is visible in that one, just the house. Now that's what I call a "before and after."

S E C R E T

WATERFALLS

Just 40 minutes from Portland, you'll find the rushing waters of **Multnomah Falls** (I-84 east), the second highest year-round waterfall in the nation. The water drops 620 feet from its origin on Larch Mountain. Unusually cold weather has been known to turn this cascade into a giant Popsicle. Timber baron Simon Benson, of Benson Bubbler fame (see "Secret Fountains"), donated the funds for the construction of the Benson Footbridge over the lower falls. Aside from enjoying the falls, you'll find trails to hike and even a restaurant, **The Lodge at Multnomah Falls** (Exit 31 off I-84, Columbia River Gorge Scenic Highway, Bridal Veil, Oregon, 503-695-2376, www.multnomahfallslodge.com), for a respite from all that activity.

Latourell Falls (Bridal Veil, Oregon, along the Columbia Gorge Scenic Highway) is at the top of a short, steep, but paved climb. The falls drop a spectacular 250 feet. It's very tempting to try to get as close to the edge as possible, but there's no railing, so be careful. *Very* careful. Most people stop at the end of the paved trail, but the path beyond is a great walk, especially for children. It gradually climbs up the east side of Latourell Creek to the less-impressive Upper Falls, and then wanders down the bank to the parking lot. In summer, it can be very crowded. Only hikers and dogs are allowed on the trails; no horses or mountain bikes are permitted. Sadly, the area is not handicapped accessible.

For a waterfall a little closer to town, see "Secret Kisses."

SECRET
WATERFRONT

Not since Marlon Brando graced the movie screen has there been such a good reason to be excited about a waterfront. Portland's **Eastbank Esplanade**, a 1.5-mile pedestrian/cycling trail that extends along the east side of downtown Portland's Willamette River from the Steel Bridge to the Hawthorne Bridge, has citizens flocking to the riverside. The esplanade includes a 1,200-foot walkway atop the Willamette River, an adjoining 120-foot public boat dock, public art, and a Steel Bridge pedestrian/cycling crossing at riverbank level. Long-term plans call for the esplanade to reach the Oregon Museum of Science and Industry to the south, and to provide additional amenities, such as a boathouse, scenic overlooks, and a park.

Want to catch the fireworks while sipping a Chardonnay? **Three Degrees** (RiverPlace, 1510 sw Harbor Way, Downtown, 503-295-6166, www.threedegreesrestaurant.com) is a bistro-ish establishment that attracts a polished crowd to its outdoor café. This place fills up fast on special occasions, so be sure to get there early for a prime seat.

Just a little out of town is **Blinn's Boathouse** (40 N State Street, Lake Oswego, Oregon, 503-636-4561). Its modest front door opens onto a nautical world. Enjoy a summer's eve on the deck with barbecue and live music, and then venture inside for light jazz and Irish coffee when the sun goes down.

S E C R E T

WEATHER

If you find yourself in Portland's "living room" (Pioneer Courthouse Square, Downtown) any day at noon, be prepared for a weather "report." The **Weather Machine**, a shiny sphere atop a 25-foot pole, plays a musical fanfare and sends forth one of three creatures, depending on the day's weather. When it's clear, you'll see the sun figure Helia; on stormy days, a dragon; and on gray, drizzly days, a great blue heron. It won't make the weather any better, but it does add some fun.

S E C R E T

WEB SITES

The Portland Oregon Visitors Association has a terrific Web site (www.travelportland.com), chock-full of information about past and present Portland. Click on "Visitor Info" for advice on sightseeing, arts, shopping, and outdoor activities, as well as for an online hotel reservation service. It also includes a comprehensive list of city events, as well as special offers on hotel prices and other tourist specials.

City Search (portland.citysearch.com) tops the list of places to search when you need up-to-the-minute information. For a comprehensive appraisal of the nightlife in the city, check out *BarFly Magazine*'s site (www.barflymag.com).

To plan your route around the city on public transit, go to the TriMet/MAX Web site at www.trimet.org, or the site for the new streetcars at www.portlandstreetcar.org.

A Web site run by the state's largest newspaper, the *Oregonian* (www.oregonlive.com), offers news updates, events calendars, local entertainment listings, and chat rooms.

Nature of the Northwest (www.naturenw.org) is a clearinghouse for information on reserving and renting public lands in the Northwest. It will also fill you in on the passes you'll need to park at trailheads and in snow parks.

Need the latest info on what's brewing? www.oregonbeer.com

Or, if your tastes run to the grape head to www.oregonwine.org, www.oregonwinecountry.org, or www.oregonwine.com.

SECRET

WHITE HOUSE

You'll feel ever so presidential when you spend a night in the **White House Bed and Breakfast** (1914 NE 22nd Avenue, Irvington, 503-287-7131 or 800-272-7131, www.portlandswhitehouse.com). With its stately Greek columns and circular drive, it bears a remarkable, if diminutive, resemblance to its East Coast counterpart. And no, it won't cost a campaign contribution to stay there.

S E C R E T

WILDLIFE

Need to get your feet wet? Mingle with flora and fauna? **Oaks Bottom Wildlife Refuge** (SE 7th Avenue and SE Sellwood Boulevard, Sellwood-Moreland, 503-823-6131, www.portlandonline.com/parks/), which began as 120-acre tract of wetland on the east bank of Willamette River, has turned into a bird-watching and wildlife paradise. Expect to spot hawks, quail, mallards, and kestrels. The real star of the show is the great blue heron, the official bird of the city of Portland. Oaks Bottom is a favorite place for these impressive birds because of its proximity to one of the rookeries on Ross Island. The neat thing about Oaks Bottom is that it's so close to the old-style amusement park. It's a secret two-for-one, combining nature and a little man-made fun.

Well worth visiting is the **Audubon Society of Portland** (5151 NW Cornell Road, Hillside, 503-292-6855, www.audubonportland.org). The 60-acre center helps rehabilitate more than 4,000 injured birds and animals a year. Many of the animals, even after recuperating, are unable to return to the wild and become permanent members of the community. In residence you'll find pygmy owls, red-tailed hawks, and an acorn woodpecker. Naturalist guides often lead tours through the sanctuary. The miles of hiking trails here link up with Forest Park (see "Secret Forests"). If you love to hike, leave your car at Lower Macleay Park (part of Forest Park, accessible by car at NW Upshur Street), and then hike up to the society's building on a one-mile dirt path. The trail follows a winding creek through an old-growth forest grove. The last part of the hike is uphill (don't say I didn't warn you), so plan on resting every once in a while and bring water.

S E C R E T

WINDSURFING
❧

Can you windsurf in Portland? You bet your board you can. Take your gear to the **Columbia River Gorge**. (Okay, it's a little outside the city, but not much.) What makes windsurfing here so terrific? Well, for starters, it's one of the most beautiful places in the world, with cascading waterfalls, mountain forests, and snow-capped volcanoes such as Mount Hood and Mount Adams in the distance. And all of this is just 30 minutes from downtown Portland.

Spring through fall, strong west winds — up to 40 miles per hour — funnel through the Cascade Range past the towns of Stevenson, Cascade Locks, Hood River, and White Salmon. These powerful winds and warm temperatures beckon windsurfers to play in the Columbia's fresh water.

Want to try and don't know how? **Big Winds** (207 Front Street, Hood River, Oregon, 541-386-6086 or 888-509-4210, www.big winds.com) offers lessons to windsurfers of all levels. It also claims to have the largest fleet of rental boards on the West Coast. Don't forget to pick up a free *Gorge Guide*. There are more than 50 approved windsurfing spots on the Columbia River, many of them right around Hood River.

A favorite location for many local windsurfers is **Rooster Rock State Park** (I-84 east to exit 25, 503-695-2261 or 800-551-6949).

This mile-long sandy beach is crowded with windsurfers when the east wind blows.

S E C R E T

YARN

Have you secretly yearned to knit one, purl two but didn't know where to begin? **Northwest Wools** (3524 SW Troy Street, Multnomah, 503-244-5024, northwestwools.com) carries the Dale of Norway "Learn to Knit Kit," which will have you purling and cabling away the hours in no time flat. If you want more than a takeaway box of instructions, then sign up for lessons. Knitting is so trendy that even Julia Roberts knits these days. The selection of wools is also superior. You may never again prowl the aisles of Michael's in search of sophisticated skeins.

If you don't know a knit from a purl but want a delightful sweater for a young child, go to **Mako** (732 NW 23rd Avenue, Northwest, 503-274-9081). Mako and her sister turn out the most marvelous sweaters, vests, and hats, all handknit from cotton.

Tucked away in The Pearl is a pearl of a knitting shop. **The Knit Knot Studio** (1238 NW Glisan Street, The Pearl, 503-222-3818, www .knitknotstudiopdx.com) has a select range of upscale yarns and patterns. But, this is the place to bring your favorite knitted garment that needs some TLC. Proprietress, Elizabeth Prusiewicz, is a whiz at knitting repairs.

SECRET

YURTS

They're round, they sleep five, and Oregon has 152 of them. A YURT (Year-round, Universal, Recreational Tent) closely resembles an Asian tent: a collapsible circular tent of skins stretched over a pole frame, long used by Central Asian nomadic peoples. Today they cover hippies, yippees, yuppies, and those who don't want to sleep in a square environment. A modern YURT is a domed tent with a plywood floor, structural wall support, electricity, and a clear, Plexiglas skylight.

A state park YURT usually measures about 16 feet in diameter and has 10-foot ceilings. Furnished with a bunk bed that sleeps three and a fold-out couch that can sleep two, a YURT is a cool way to take the family camping. Bring your own sleeping bag and bedding, flashlight, cooking and eating utensils, and water container. Each site has its own fire ring and picnic tables. You'll find them in state parks in the Portland area as far south as Coos Bay on the Pacific coast, and to the north in Tillamook (800-452-5687). Cost is $25 a night, plus a $6 reservation fee.

SECRET FUTURE

No tour guide can be definitively comprehensive, especially when the aim is to uncover those hidden places that have previously escaped notice. Undoubtedly, some worthwhile attractions have remained hidden even from our best efforts to ferret them out.

In the interest of our own self-improvement, we ask readers to let us know of the places they've unearthed that they believe warrant inclusion in future editions of *Secret Portland, Oregon*. If we use your suggestion, we'll send you a free copy on publication. Please contact us at the following address:

Secret Portland, Oregon
c/o ECW PRESS

2120 Queen Street East, Suite 200
Toronto, Ontario, Canada M4E 1E2

Or e-mail us at: info@ecwpress.com

PHOTO SITES

SUBJECT INDEX

LOCATION INDEX

ALPHABETICAL INDEX